GIFTED AND TALENTED TEST PREPARATION

COGAT® GRADE 5

370+ Questions /
2 Full-Length Practice Tests
Level 11

Savant Test Prep™
www.SavantPrep.com

Please leave a review for this book!

Thank you for purchasing this resource.

If you would take a moment to kindly leave a
review on the website where you purchased this publication,
we would greatly appreciate it.

TABLE OF CONTENTS

INTRODUCTION

COGAT® GENERAL INFORMATION

- COGAT® stands for Cognitive Abilities Test®. It measures students' reasoning skills and problem-solving skills.
- It provides the teachers and administrators at your child's school with an assessment of your child's cognitive skills.
    - The test is sometimes used together with the ITBS™ (a.k.a. Iowa Test) to measure academic achievement.
- It is commonly used as a screener for gifted and talented programs.
    - Gifted and Talented (G&T) selection sometimes requires a teacher recommendation as well.
- The test is usually administered in a group setting.
- A teacher (or other school associate) administers the test, reading the directions. (Computerized versions of the test are also available.)
- Please check with your school / testing site regarding its testing procedures, as these may differ.

COGAT® LEVEL 11 FORMAT

- Students in fifth grade take the COGAT® Level 11.
- The test has 176 questions.
- The test is divided into 3 main parts, each called a "Battery." Each Battery has three question types. The chart below lists the number of questions by question type. (The two practice tests in this book have *approximately* this number of questions.)

VERBAL BATTERY	NON-VERBAL BATTERY	QUANTITATIVE BATTERY
Verbal Classification: 20 Questions	Figure Classification: 22 Questions	Number Puzzles: 16 Questions
Verbal Analogies: 24 Questions	Figure Analogies: 22 Questions	Number Series: 18 Questions
Sentence Completion: 20 Questions	Paper Folding: 16 Questions	Number Analogies: 18 Questions

- Often, schools administer one Battery per day, allowing approximately 45 minutes per Battery.
- Students have around 15 minutes to complete each question type (for example, students would have around 15 minutes to complete Verbal Analogies).
- See pages 6-11 for examples and explanations of each question type.

COGAT® SCORING

- Students receive points for correct answers. Points are not deducted for incorrect answers. (Therefore, students should at least guess versus leaving a question blank.)
- In general, schools have a "cut-off" COGAT® score, which they consider together with additional criteria, for gifted & talented acceptance. This varies by school.
- This score is usually at least 98%. (However, some schools accept scores 95% or even 85%.)
- A score of 98% means that your child scored as well as, or better than, 98% of children in his/her testing group.
- COGAT® scores are available for the entire test and can be broken down by Battery.
- Depending on the school/program, such a "cut-off" score may only be required on one or two of the Batteries (and not on the test overall).
- It is essential to check with your school/program for their acceptance procedures.
    - (The COGAT® Practice Tests in this book can not yield these percentiles because they have not been given to a large enough group of students to produce an accurate comparison / calculation.)

HOW TO USE THIS BOOK

1. Go over examples and explanations (p.6 - 11).

2. Do Practice Test 1.
- Unless your child has already completed COGAT®-prep questions before, then you should do these questions together with your child.
  - Talk about what the question is asking your child to do.
- Questions progress in difficulty.
  - The first few questions are quite simple.
- Do at least one section (Verbal / Non-Verbal/ Quantitative) per day.
- Do not assign a time limit.
- Go over the answers using the Answer Key.
  - For questions missed, go over the answers again, discussing what makes the correct answer better than the other choices.

3. Do Practice Test 2.
- If your child progressed easily through Practice Test 1, then see how well your child can do on Practice Test 2 without your help.
- If your child needed assistance with much of Practice Test 1, then continue to assist your child with Practice Test 2.
- Do at least one section (Verbal / Non-Verbal/ Quantitative) per day.
- If you wish to assign a time limit, assign around 15 minutes per question type.
- Go over the answers using the Answer Key.
  - For questions missed, go over the answers again, discussing what makes the correct answer better than the other choices.

4. Go to our website, www.SavantPrep.com, for FREE 10 bonus practice questions (PDF format).

GET FREE 10 BONUS PRACTICE QUESTIONS (PDF)!
GO TO WWW.SAVANTPREP.COM AND GET THEM TODAY.

TEST-TAKING TIPS

- Ensure your child listens carefully to the directions.
- Make sure (s)he does not rush through questions. (There is no prize for finishing first!) Tell your child to look carefully at the question. Then, tell your child to look at each answer choice before marking his/her answer.
  - If you notice your child continuing to rush through the questions, tell him/her to point to each part of the question. Then, point to each answer choice.
- If (s)he does not know the answer, then use the process of elimination. Cross out any answer choices which are clearly incorrect, then choose from those remaining.
- This tip/suggestion is entirely at your discretion. You may wish to offer some sort of special motivation to encourage your child to do his/her best. An extra incentive of, for example, an art set, a building block set, or a special outing can go a long way in motivating young learners!
- The night before testing, it is imperative that children have enough sleep, without any interruptions. (Think about the difference in your brain function with a good night's sleep vs. without. The same goes for your child's brain function.)
- The morning before the test, ensure your child eats a healthy breakfast with protein and complex carbs. Do not let them eat sugar, chocolate, etc.
- If you can choose the time your child will take the test (for example, if (s)he will take the test individually, instead of at school with a group), opt for a morning testing session, when your child will be most alert.

QUESTION EXAMPLES

- Here is an overview of the nine COGAT® question types.
- This section has <u>very simple</u> examples, to introduce test concepts.
    - Do these examples together with your child. Read him/her the directions.
- Below the questions are explanations for parents.

1. VERBAL ANALOGIES (VERBAL BATTERY)

- **Directions (read to child):** Here are two sets of words. Look at the first set of words. Try to see how they belong together. Then, look at the next set of words. The question mark shows where the answer is missing. Can you see which answer choice would make the second set of words go together in the same way that the first set of words goes together?

scales → fish : feathers → ?   A. pen   B. shark   C. beak   D. bird   E. fly

- **Explanation (for parents):** Your child must figure out how the first set is related and belongs together. Then, (s)he must figure out which answer choice would go with the first word of the second set so that the second set would have the same analogous relationship as the first set. (The small arrows demonstrate that the words go together.)

- One strategy is to try to define a "rule" to describe how the first set belongs together. Then, take this "rule" and use it with the second set. Look at the answer choices, and figure out which answer would make the second set follow your "rule."

- **Using the above question as an example, say to your child:**
In this question, we have "scales" and "fish." Scales are part of a fish. Also, more specifically, scales cover a fish. A rule would be, "the first thing covers the second thing." In the second set we have "feathers." Let's try the answer choices with our rule. A pen is not correct nor is a shark or a beak. "Bird" is correct because feathers cover a bird.

- Another similar strategy is to try to come up with a sentence to describe how the first set belongs together. Then, use this sentence with the second word. Look at the answer choices, and figure out which answer would make the sentence work with this second set. With both strategies, if more than one answer choice works, then you need a more specific rule/ sentence.

- Make sure your child does not choose an answer simply because it *has to do with* the previous words or reminds them of previous words. In the above example, "beak" *has to do with* "feathers." "Shark" may *remind* them of the second word in the first set, "fish." These types of words are sometimes included in the answer choices, and students who do not look carefully at the question may choose them by mistake.

- The table below outlines the logic used in verbal analogies (on the COGAT®, as well as in verbal analogies, in general). We suggest reading the questions and answer choices to your child. This will help familiarize him/her with analogy logic.

Question (say below & each 'Choice' to child)	Choice 1	Choice 2	Choice 3	Choice 4	Analogy Logic
1. Fish -is to- Aquarium as Bird -is to- ?	Bowl	Butterfly	Cage ✓	Nest (note logic)	Pet: Pet's Home (Made by People)
2. Acorns -are to- Squirrel as Seeds -are to- ?	Grass	Bird ✓	Fish	Snake	Animal: Animal's Food
3. Calf -is to- Cow as Cub -is to- ?	Tiger ✓	Horse	Goose	Bull	Baby: Adult
4. Lion -is to- Fur as Snake -is to- ?	Lizard	Hair	Fangs	Scales ✓	Animal: Animal's Covering
5. Happy -is to- Sad as Wet -is to- ?	Damp	Clean	Water	Dry ✓	Antonyms
6. Tiger -is to- Cheetah as Butterfly -is to- ?	Bird	Bat	Moth ✓	Jaguar	Similar Animals
7. Small -is to- Little as Afraid -is to- ?	Dark	Tired	Haunted	Scared ✓	Synonyms

Question (say below & each 'Choice' to child)	Choice 1	Choice 2	Choice 3	Choice 4	Analogy Logic
8. Flower -is to- Bouquet as Kernel -is to- ?	Snack	Plant	Corn Cob ✓	Crop	Part: Whole
9. Ship -is to- Port as Car -is to- ?	Truck	Garage ✓	Marina	Wheel	Object: Location
10. Pencil -is to- Paper as Paint -is to- ?	Wall ✓	Color	Red	Light	Object: Object Used With
11. Lumber -is to- Fence as Paper -is to- ?	Log	Branch	Tree	Book ✓	Object: Product That Object Is Put Together To Make
12. Doctor -is to- Stethoscope as Carpenter -is to- ?	Boot	Builder	Cabinet	Hammer ✓	Worker Who Uses Object: Object
13. Cheese -is to- Refrigerator as Ice -is to- ?	Snow	Toaster	Freezer ✓	Cube	Object: Item Used to Store/Hold Object
14. Box -is to- Cube as Globe -is to- ?	Prism	Sphere ✓	Oval	Pentagon	Object: Similar Shape
15. Straw -is to- Juice as Spoon -is to- ?	Cereal ✓	Salad	Steak	Sandwich	Utensil: Object Utensil Is Used With
16. Egg -is to- Chicken as Milk -is to- ?	Chick	Cheese	Rooster	Cow ✓	Food/Drink: Source of Food/Drink
17. Large -is to- Enormous as Good -is to- ?	Bad	So-So	Happy	Super ✓	Degree

2. VERBAL CLASSIFICATION (VERBAL BATTERY)

• **Directions (read to child):** The three words in the top row are alike in some way. Look at the bottom row. There are five words. Which word in the bottom row goes best with the three words in the top row?

red   green   blue

A. paint   B. color   C. white   D. rainbow   E. shade

• **Explanation (for parents):** Together with your child, try to figure out a "rule" describing how the top words are alike and belong together. Then, apply the "rule" to each answer choice to determine which one follows it. If your child finds that more than one choice follows the rule, then a more specific rule is needed.

• **Using the above question as an example, say to your child:** In the top row, we have "red," "green," and "blue." What do these have in common? Each of these are colors. This is how they are alike. Which answer choice follows this rule of "colors?" The only answer choice that does is "white."

• Make sure your child does not choose a word simply because the choice *has to do with* the top three. For example, the other choices, especially Choice B ("color") have to do with the top three. However, "white" is the only choice that actually follows the rule.

Here is another example to demonstrate the importance of "rules" that are *specific*.

Atlantic   Indian   Arctic

A. American   B. Caribbean Sea   C. Gulf of Mexico   D. Pacific   E. ocean

In this example, the correct rule is "oceans of the world." (The world's oceans are the: Atlantic, Pacific, Arctic, Indian, and Southern.) However, a test-taker may at first come up with the rule "large body of water." If this happens, (s)he would have more than one answer choice that could be correct (Caribbean Sea, Gulf of Mexico, or Pacific). In this case, a more specific rule is needed. Here, (s)he should read the top three words again. In doing so, (s)he may realize that the top three words are large bodies of water that are *also* oceans. A more specific rule would be "ocean" or "oceans of the world." Therefore, the correct answer would be Choice D, "Pacific."

• Below are additional simple examples to introduce your child to classification logic. These will help familiarize him/her with basic classification logic. The classification logic/explanation is in the third column.

-Step 1: Read the three words on the left to your child. Tell him/her that these words belong together in some way.

-Step 2: Read the four words on the right to your child. Ask him/her which one of these goes best with the first three words. The answer has a check (✓). Following is a brief explanation of the question's logic in *italics*.

Question (read to child)	Answer Choices (read to child)	*Classification Logic / Explanation*
1. Cave / Hive / Web	Spider / Nest ✓ / Vet / Bat	*Animal Homes*
2. Butterfly / Ant / Bee	Worm / Horse / Bird / Dragonfly ✓	*Animal Types (Insects)*
3. Forest / Jungle / Desert	Tree / Valley / Rainforest ✓ / City	*Habitats*
4. Lemon / Grape / Apple	Strawberry ✓ / Farm / Sweet / Lettuce	*Kinds of Food (Fruit)*
5. Scientist / Nurse / Detective	Superhero / Teenager / Pilot ✓ / Fairy	*Jobs*
6. Sock / Skate / Boot	Slipper ✓ / Cap / Mitten / Toe	*Clothes/Shoes (Worn On Feet)*
7. Jet / Hot Air Balloon / Helicopter	Ship / Airport / Bird / Airplane ✓	*Transportation (Air Travel)*
8. Ruler / Scale / Measuring Tape	Thermometer ✓ / Number / TV / Pen	*Object Use (Used to Measure)*
9. Pillow / Blanket / Mattress	Towel / Chair / Sheet ✓ / Table	*Object Location (Found on Beds)*
10. Fire / Sun / Stove	Cookie / Toaster ✓ / Beach / Camp	*Object Characteristics (Give Heat)*
11. Planet / Ball / Globe	Country / Goal / Bubble ✓ / Racetrack	*Object Shape (Spherical)*

3. SENTENCE COMPLETION (VERBAL BATTERY)

• **Directions (read to child):** First, read the sentence. There is a missing word. Which answer choice goes best in the sentence? (Read the sentences and choices to your child. They may read along silently.)

As the water slowly evaporated, the bird bath became _____.
A. wet   B. empty   C. full   D. damp   E. clean

• **Explanation** Here, your child must use the information in the question and make inferences (i.e., make a best guess based on the information) and choose the *best* answer choice to fill in the blank.

• Note that Sentence Completion questions do not solely test vocabulary, but reasoning skills as well.

• Make sure your child pays close attention to every word in the sentence and to every answer choice. Have him/her re-read the complete sentence with the answer choice to ensure their choice makes the *most* sense compared to the other choices (the answer is B).

• Tell him/her to pay special attention to "negative" words like "not" or "no." Also, (s)he should watch out for words like "though," "although," "even though," which would show contrasting ideas.

4. FIGURE ANALOGIES (NON-VERBAL BATTERY)

• **Directions (read to child):** The pictures in the top boxes go together in some way. Look at the bottom boxes. One box is empty. Look at the row of pictures next to the boxes. These are the answer choices. Which one of these choices goes with the picture in the bottom box like the pictures in the top box go together?

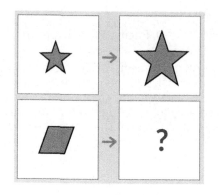

- **Explanation:** In the directions, the word "picture" means a "figure" consisting of one or more shapes/lines/etc. As with Verbal Analogies, try to define a "rule" to describe how the top set belongs together. With Figure Analogies, however, make your "rule" describe a "change" that occurs from the top left box to the top right box. Next, take this "rule" describing the change, and apply it to the bottom picture. Then, look at the answer choices to determine which one would make the bottom set also follow your "rule."

- **Using the question on the previous page, say to your child:** In the top left box, we see 1 star. In the top right box, we also see a star, but it has gotten bigger. Let's come up with a rule to describe how the picture has changed from left to right. From left to right, the shape gets bigger. On the bottom is a parallelogram. Let's look at the answer choices and see if any fit our rule. The first choice does not - the shape is smaller. The second choice does not - the shape is the same size. The third choice does not - it is a different shape. The last choice does - it is the same shape as the bottom box, but it is bigger.

- Below are examples of basic "changes" seen in Figure Analogies. Basic questions, like the example and #1-#9 below, have one "change." While more advanced questions have two changes (or changes that are not as obvious). The questions in the book's two practice tests will be much more challenging than these. See if your child can explain the changes below. At the end is a brief explanation.

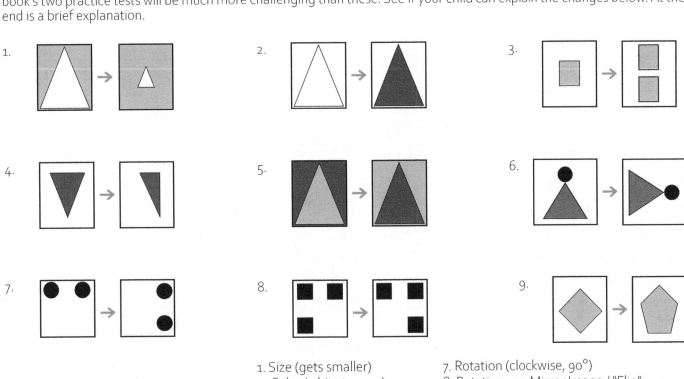

1. Size (gets smaller)
2. Color (white to gray)
3. Quantity (plus 1)
4. Whole to Half
5. Color Reversal
6. Rotation (clockwise, 90°)
7. Rotation (clockwise, 90°)
8. Rotation -or- Mirror Image / "Flip"
9. Number of Shape Sides (shape with +1 side)
10. Two Changes: Rotation (clockwise, 90°)
    and Color Reversal

5. FIGURE CLASSIFICATION (NON-VERBAL BATTERY)

- **Directions   (read to child):** The top row shows three pictures that are alike in some way. Look at the bottom row. There are four pictures. Which picture in the bottom row goes best with the pictures in the top row?

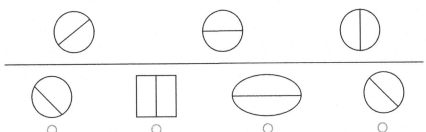

- **Explanation (for parents):** Together with your child, try to figure out a "rule" describing how the top pictures are alike and belong together. Then, apply the "rule" to each answer choice to determine which one follows it. If your child finds that more than one choice follows the rule, then a more specific rule is needed.

Here we see 3 circles. These circles are all divided in half. What is a rule that describes how they are alike? They are all circles that are divided in half. In the bottom row, which choice follows this rule? Choice 1 is a circle, but it's not divided in half. Choice 2 and 3 are divided in half, but they are not circles. Choice 4 is a circle divided in half. Choice 4 is the answer.

This list outlines some basic logic used in Figure Classification questions. (Practice test questions will be more challenging.)

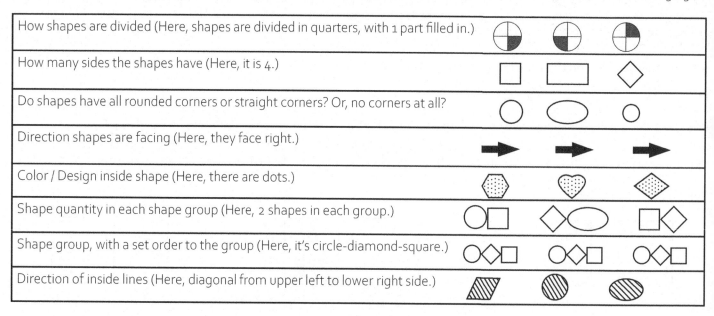

How shapes are divided (Here, shapes are divided in quarters, with 1 part filled in.)	
How many sides the shapes have (Here, it is 4.)	
Do shapes have all rounded corners or straight corners? Or, no corners at all?	
Direction shapes are facing (Here, they face right.)	
Color / Design inside shape (Here, there are dots.)	
Shape quantity in each shape group (Here, 2 shapes in each group.)	
Shape group, with a set order to the group (Here, it's circle-diamond-square.)	
Direction of inside lines (Here, diagonal from upper left to lower right side.)	

6. PAPER FOLDING (NON-VERBAL BATTERY)

• **Directions (read to child):** The top row of pictures shows a sheet of paper. The paper was folded, then something was cut out. Which picture in the bottom row shows how the paper would look after its unfolded?

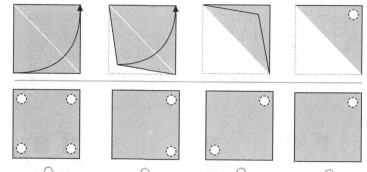

• **Explanation (read to child):** The first choice has too many holes. In the second choice, the holes are not in the correct position. The third choice has the correct number of holes and in the correct position. The last choice only shows the hole on top.

• **Tip:** It is common for children to initially struggle with Paper Folding - it is not an activity most children have much experience with. First, have a look at these Paper Folding examples. Then, demonstrate using real paper and scissors.

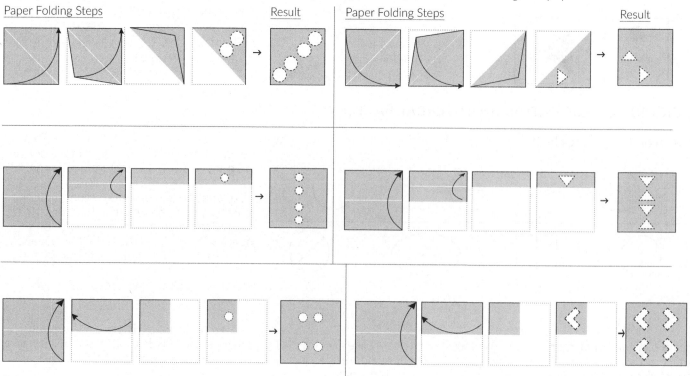

Paper Folding Steps — Result   Paper Folding Steps — Result

7. NUMBER SERIES (QUANTITATIVE BATTERY)

• **Directions (read to child):** The top row of numbers have made a pattern. Which answer choice would complete the pattern?

| 6 | 9 | 12 | 15 | 18 | ? |

A. 21   B. 3   C. 22   D. 24   E. 30

• **Explanation:** To help your child see the pattern, ask them to write the difference between each number and the next. Here, the difference between 6 and 9 is 3. The difference between 9 and 12 is 3. The difference between 12 and 15 is 3, and so on. In less challenging questions, this "difference" will be the same for each set of numbers. If the pattern is "add 3," then the answer is 21, because 18 +3 = 21. In more challenging questions, this pattern is not consistent with each set of numbers. See below:

30	29	27	24	20	15	?	Pattern: -1, -2, -3, -4, etc.; Answer: 9
7	2	1	7	2	1	?	Pattern: 7-2-1; Answer: 7
3	4	6	7	9	10	?	Pattern: +1, +2, +1, +2, etc.; Answer: 12
5	0	6	0	7	0	?	Pattern: every other number +1; every other number = 0; Answer: 8.

8. NUMBER PUZZLES (QUANTITATIVE BATTERY)

• **Directions:** Which number would be in place of the question mark so that both sides of the equal sign are the same?

• **Explanation:** These questions have two formats. The first example is a standard math problem. In the second example, your child needs to replace the black shape with the given number. Should your child have problems figuring out the answer of either format, (s)he can simply test each answer choice until they find the correct answer.

1. $19 = ? + 5$ A. 5   B. 24   C. 20   D. 4   E. 14

2. $? = \blacklozenge - 8$ A. 0   B. 1   C. 2   D. 3   E. 4

      $\blacklozenge = 11$

9. NUMBER ANALOGIES (QUANTITATIVE BATTERY)

• **Directions:** Look at the first two sets of numbers. Come up with a rule that both of these sets follow. Use this rule to figure out which answer choice goes in place of the question mark in the last set of numbers.

$[2 \rightarrow 6]$ $[4 \rightarrow 12]$ $[10 \rightarrow ?]$ A. 6   B. 3   C. 13   D. 30   E. 7

• **Explanation (read to child):** Have your child figure out a rule that explains how the first number "changes" into the second number. It could use addition, subtraction, multiplication, or division. Have him/her write the rule by *each* pair. (S)he must make sure this rule works with *both* pairs. The rule is "multiply by 3", so 30 is the answer.

-PRACTICE TEST 1 BEGINS ON THE NEXT PAGE-

VERBAL CLASSIFICATION

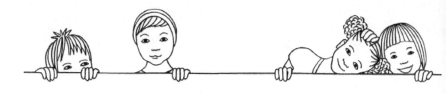

Directions (Read these aloud to your child. Your child may read along silently): The top row has three words that are alike in some way. In the bottom row are five words. Which word in the bottom row goes best with the words in the top row?

Explanation (for parents): A more detailed explanation and another Verbal Classification example question is on p.7. If you have not already, look over p.7 (later). Following is an excerpt. Together with your child, try to figure out a "rule" describing how the top words are alike and belong together. Then, apply the "rule" to each answer choice to determine which one follows it. If your child finds that more than one choice follows the rule, then a more specific rule is needed.

Example (read to child): In the top row are the words "cougar," "leopard," and "panther." Let's come up with a "rule" to describe how these are each alike or how they belong together. These are all types of animals. Now, let's find the answer choice on the bottom that follows this same rule. Looking at the answer choices, we see that more than one choice could be correct. When this happens, we need a rule that's more specific.

If we look at the three top words again, we see that all these are types of cats. Let's try this rule. Which one of the choices is a cat? "Jaguar" follows our rule because it is a cat.

1   **cougar**   **leopard**   **panther**

    Ⓐ animal   Ⓑ bear   Ⓒ giraffe   Ⓓ elephant   Ⓔ jaguar

2   **heart**   **stomach**   **lungs**

    Ⓐ air   Ⓑ brain   Ⓒ body   Ⓓ organ   Ⓔ blood

3 atlas   autobiography   newspaper

    Ⓐ fantasy   Ⓑ legend   Ⓒ summary   Ⓓ fable   Ⓔ dictionary

4 finish   complete   conclude

    Ⓐ end   Ⓑ distant   Ⓒ departure   Ⓓ base   Ⓔ leave

5 unlike   contrasting   dissimilar

    Ⓐ duplicate   Ⓑ prior   Ⓒ different   Ⓓ distant   Ⓔ former

6 African   South American   Australian

    Ⓐ Continent   Ⓑ Russian   Ⓒ Nation   Ⓓ Asian   Ⓔ Egyptian

7 minute   decade   year

    Ⓐ hour   Ⓑ calendar   Ⓒ watch   Ⓓ centimeter   Ⓔ gallon

8 butter   pollen   egg yolk

    Ⓐ eggshell   Ⓑ stem   Ⓒ school bus   Ⓓ milk   Ⓔ yogurt

9 volleyball   globe   marble

    Ⓐ clock   Ⓑ planet   Ⓒ checkerboard   Ⓓ map   Ⓔ net

10 lessen   decrease   shorten

    Ⓐ increase   Ⓑ equal   Ⓒ reduce   Ⓓ outline   Ⓔ strengthen

11 aisle   hallway   trail

    Ⓐ hike   Ⓑ avenue   Ⓒ freeway   Ⓓ driveway   Ⓔ path

12 scarce   limited   sparse

    (A) lacking   (B) sufficient   (C) satisfactory   (D) tolerable   (E) precise

13 descend   collapse   sink

    (A) climb   (B) dive   (C) float   (D) swim   (E) layer

14 soaked   soggy   dripping

    (A) foggy   (B) humid   (C) drenched   (D) rain   (E) moist

15 basement   vault   cavern

    (A) field   (B) terrain   (C) attic   (D) cellar   (E) mountain

16 opponent   competitor   rival

    (A) coach   (B) partner   (C) umpire   (D) contest   (E) challenger

17 chest   cabinet   garage

    (A) locker   (B) door   (C) vehicle   (D) table   (E) microwave

18 country   continent   town

    (A) house   (B) mayor   (C) president   (D) state   (E) capitol

19 painter   electrician   plumber

    (A) gardener   (B) carpenter   (C) miner   (D) farmer   (E) lawyer

20 always   often   seldom

    (A) late   (B) early   (C) probably   (D) likely   (E) frequently

VERBAL ANALOGIES

Directions (Read these aloud to your child. Your child may read along silently): The first set of words goes together in some way. In the second set of words, the answer is missing. You must figure out which answer choice would make the second set of words go together in the same way that the first set of words goes together.

Explanation (for parents): A more detailed explanation and another example question is on p.6. If you have not already, look over p.6 (later). Following is an excerpt. Your child must figure out how the first set of words is related and belongs together. Then, (s)he must figure out which answer choice would make the second set have the same relationship as the first set.

Example (read this to child): "Drum" and "instrument." These are the words in the first set. (Together, try to come up with a "rule" describing how they are alike and go together.) A drum is a type of instrument. The first word is a type of the second word. Let's try this rule. Let's look at the first word in the second set: "horse." Remembering our rule, which choice goes best with "horse?" Let's look at our answer choices. A horse is a type of mammal, so that is our answer. Choice C.

1   **drum → instrument : horse →**

   Ⓐ stable   Ⓑ breed   Ⓒ mammal   Ⓓ pony   Ⓔ cow

2   **letter → word : sentence →**

   Ⓐ atlas   Ⓑ letters   Ⓒ predicate   Ⓓ subject   Ⓔ paragraph

3   **foot → mile : day →**

   Ⓐ Monday   Ⓑ year   Ⓒ noon   Ⓓ hour   Ⓔ minute

4   **dishes → cabinet : hay →**

   Ⓐ barn   Ⓑ harvest   Ⓒ wheat   Ⓓ tractor   Ⓔ field

5   **ceiling → sealing : Greece →**

     Ⓐ geese   Ⓑ fleece   Ⓒ green   Ⓓ grease   Ⓔ greed

6   **red → yellow : happy →**

     Ⓐ good   Ⓑ great   Ⓒ smile   Ⓓ orange   Ⓔ cheerful

7   **rapid → swift : unusual →**

     Ⓐ unimportant   Ⓑ bizarre   Ⓒ regular   Ⓓ exciting   Ⓔ interesting

8   **color → colorful : water →**

     Ⓐ wet   Ⓑ arid   Ⓒ thirsty   Ⓓ dehydrated   Ⓔ evaporated

9   **scientist → experiment : detective →**

     Ⓐ mystery   Ⓑ thief   Ⓒ badge   Ⓓ investigation   Ⓔ crime

10   **sundial → clock : abacus →**

     Ⓐ beads   Ⓑ calculator   Ⓒ measuring tape   Ⓓ addition   Ⓔ compass

11   **peach → pit : Earth →**

     Ⓐ continent   Ⓑ planet   Ⓒ crust   Ⓓ core   Ⓔ magma

12   **silver → gold : helium →**

     Ⓐ fuel   Ⓑ element   Ⓒ jewelry   Ⓓ balloon   Ⓔ oxygen

13   **equal → equivalent : adequate →**

     Ⓐ sufficient   Ⓑ inadequate   Ⓒ aide   Ⓓ appreciate   Ⓔ alike

14   accept → reject : decline →

    Ⓐ pause   Ⓑ decrease   Ⓒ recline   Ⓓ incline   Ⓔ pass

15   drawer → reward : loots →

    Ⓐ tools   Ⓑ stool   Ⓒ tolls   Ⓓ stools   Ⓔ toll

16   jacket → sleeve : tree →

    Ⓐ forest   Ⓑ orchard   Ⓒ oak   Ⓓ bark   Ⓔ branch

17   social studies → geography : science →

    Ⓐ biology   Ⓑ history   Ⓒ biologist   Ⓓ experiment   Ⓔ astronomer

18   chain → link : fence →

    Ⓐ yard   Ⓑ house   Ⓒ protection   Ⓓ board   Ⓔ wall

19   settler → settlement : ship →

    Ⓐ cargo   Ⓑ crew   Ⓒ dock   Ⓓ vessel   Ⓔ fleet

20   dirt → clean : weight →

    Ⓐ pounds   Ⓑ scale   Ⓒ heavy   Ⓓ light   Ⓔ strong

21   numerical → number : chronological →

    Ⓐ time   Ⓑ location   Ⓒ calendar   Ⓓ timeline   Ⓔ measurement

22   wheel → bicycle : performer →

    Ⓐ actor   Ⓑ acting   Ⓒ cinema   Ⓓ director   Ⓔ duo

SENTENCE COMPLETION

Directions (Read these aloud to your child.):

In each question there is a missing word. First, read the sentence. Then, look below the sentence at each of the answer choices. Which choice would go best in the sentence?

Additional information (for parents): Page 8 provides Sentence Completion tips. If you haven't already, read p. 8. Like the other Verbal Battery sections, this section tests *reasoning skills.* This section, although it has a fill-in-the-blank format, is not purely a vocabulary test. You will find that some of the vocabulary used in the questions is actually rather simple. Advanced vocabulary skills will certainly help with this section, but reasoning skills are also tested in this section.

1   **The town's population is around 5,000, but this number is only an _____, not an exact count.**

    Ⓐ equation   Ⓑ opinion   Ⓒ estimate   Ⓓ effect   Ⓔ index

2   **At the beginning of the play, the narrator will read the _____.**

    Ⓐ introduction Ⓑ conclusion   Ⓒ outcome   Ⓓ completion Ⓔ finale

3 I do not want the bread to be sweet, so I will _____ sugar when making the dough.

Ⓐ add   Ⓑ double   Ⓒ blend   Ⓓ utilize   Ⓔ omit

4 Without _____ evidence proving the man robbed the bank, the judge will allow him to go free.

Ⓐ weak   Ⓑ persuasive   Ⓒ unclear   Ⓓ questionable   Ⓔ uncertain

5 To prevent deer from eating her vegetables, the farmer found that a tall fence was the _____.

Ⓐ punishment   Ⓑ proof   Ⓒ reward   Ⓓ solution   Ⓔ encouragement

6 While we do not have a set date for the event, we do have a _____ one.

Ⓐ tentative   Ⓑ permanent   Ⓒ certain   Ⓓ endless   Ⓔ constant

7   The general who gave valuable military information to our enemy is guilty of _____.

(A) secrecy   (B) patriotism   (C) silence   (D) loyalty   (E) treason

8   To ensure the winner's name is chosen fairly, our teacher will pull a _____ piece of paper out of a hat.

(A) particular   (B) planned   (C) programmed   (D) random   (E) definite

9   Before telephones, telegraphs were used to _____ information.

(A) conceal   (B) translate   (C) transmit   (D) analyze   (E) categorize

10   To _____ a person's identity, we use driver's licenses or passports.

(A) verify   (B) deny   (C) reject   (D) disguise   (E) limit

11   If the plant receives an _____ amount water, its leaves will dry up.

Ⓐ enough   Ⓑ inadequate   Ⓒ abundant   Ⓓ unequal   Ⓔ ample

12   While not identical to ice cream, frozen yogurt is a tasty_____.

Ⓐ alternative   Ⓑ ingredient   Ⓒ element   Ⓓ recipe   Ⓔ factor

13   A lack of patience is a _____ when playing chess.

Ⓐ preference   Ⓑ goal   Ⓒ strategy   Ⓓ position   Ⓔ disadvantage

14   She is _____ of concentrating for long periods, so completing a 1,000-piece puzzle is no problem.

Ⓐ capable   Ⓑ incapable   Ⓒ unable   Ⓓ ineffective   Ⓔ critical

15   We need to _____ the event to a later date.

Ⓐ advance   Ⓑ continue   Ⓒ maintain   Ⓓ postpone   Ⓔ achieve

16   Cassette players, CD players, and typewriters are examples of technology that have become _____.

(A) advanced   (B) necessary   (C) obsolete   (D) current   (E) modern

17   Even though tomatoes are common in Italian food, they did not _____ in Europe.

(A) expand   (B) originate   (C) produce   (D) cease   (E) grow

18   For the garden to _____, it will need good soil and regular watering.

(A) recede   (B) decline   (C) prosper   (D) wither   (E) halt

19   You have two _____ choices that have little in common.

(A) similar   (B) related   (C) identical   (D) connected   (E) distinct

20   She chose a _____ place on the wall above her desk to display her award.

(A) covert   (B) low   (C) modest   (D) prominent   (E) subtle

FIGURE CLASSIFICATION

Directions (read to child):

The top row shows three pictures that are alike in some way. Look at the bottom row. There are five pictures. Which picture in the bottom row goes best with the pictures in the top row?

Explanation (for parents):

A more detailed explanation of Figure Classification questions is on p.9. If you have not already, look over p.9 (later). Following is an excerpt. Together with your child, try to figure out a "rule" describing how the top pictures are alike and belong together. Then, apply the "rule" to each answer choice to determine which one follows it. If your child finds that more than one choice follows the rule, then a more specific rule is needed.

Example (read to child):

Let's look at the pictures on the top row. We see 3 shape groups. In each shape group there is a larger outer shape. Inside this shape are 2 smaller squares. These smaller squares are the same color. Perhaps this could be our rule: inside the larger shape are two smaller squares that are the same color. However, looking at our answer choices, we see three choices would follow this rule. So, we need a more specific rule. Looking again at the figures on the top row, we notice that the two squares are aligned vertically AND the two squares are the same color. Looking again at the answer choices, we see that choice D follows this rule.

1

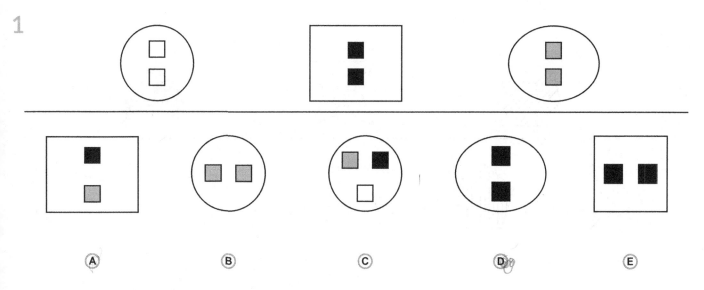

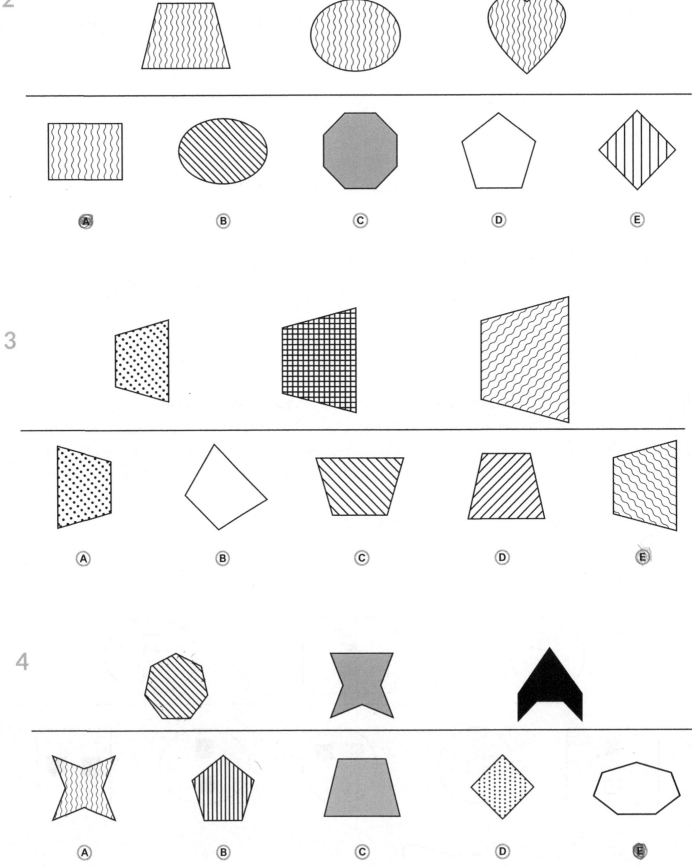

2

A B C D E

3

A B C D E

4

A B C D E

24

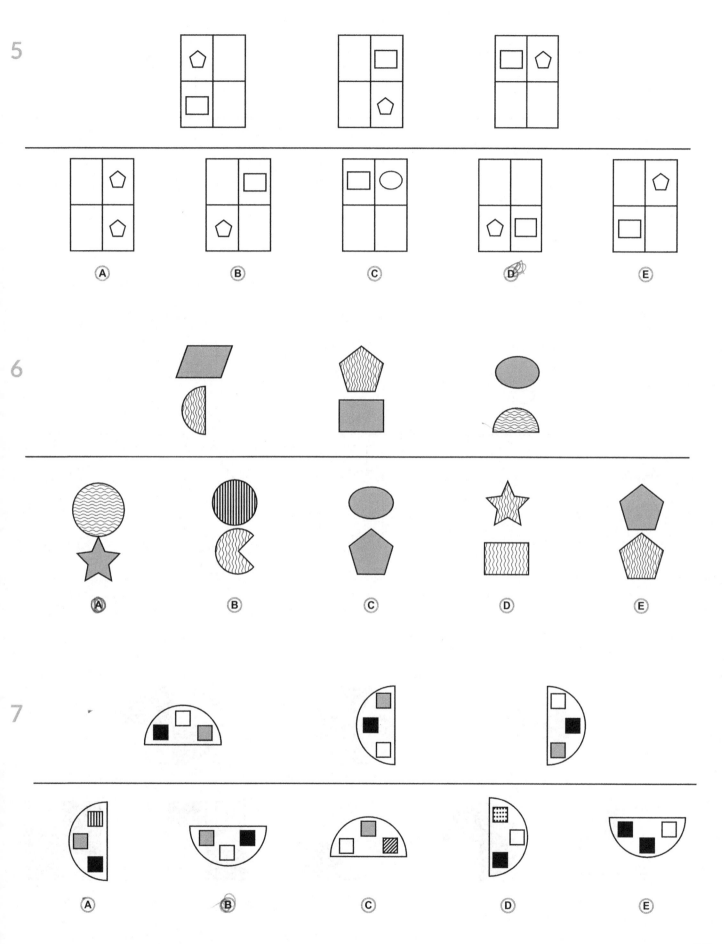

8

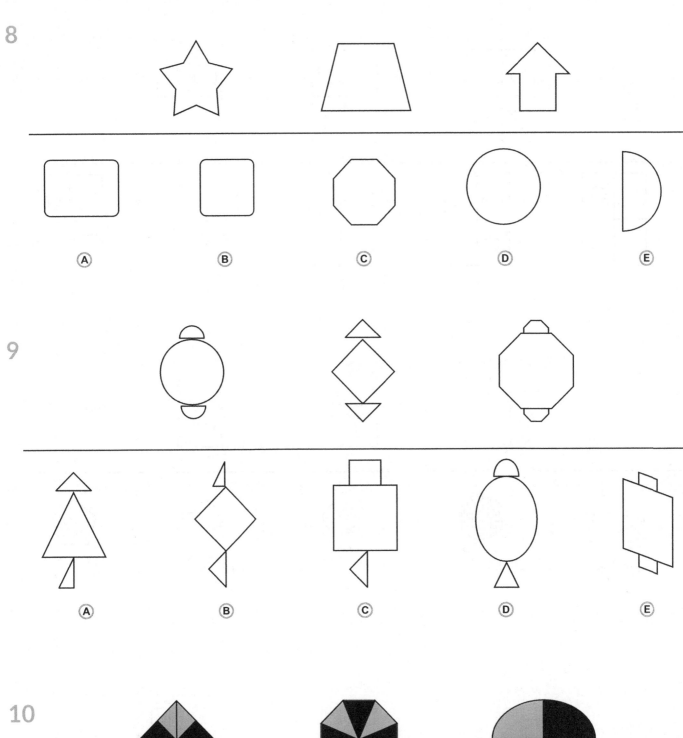

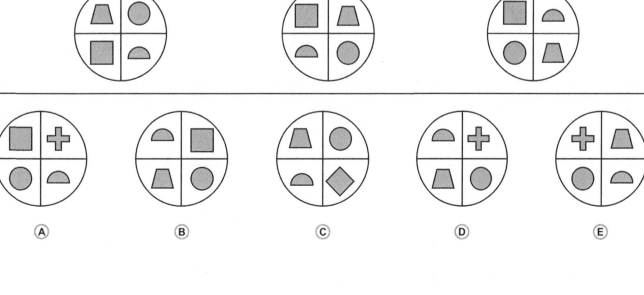

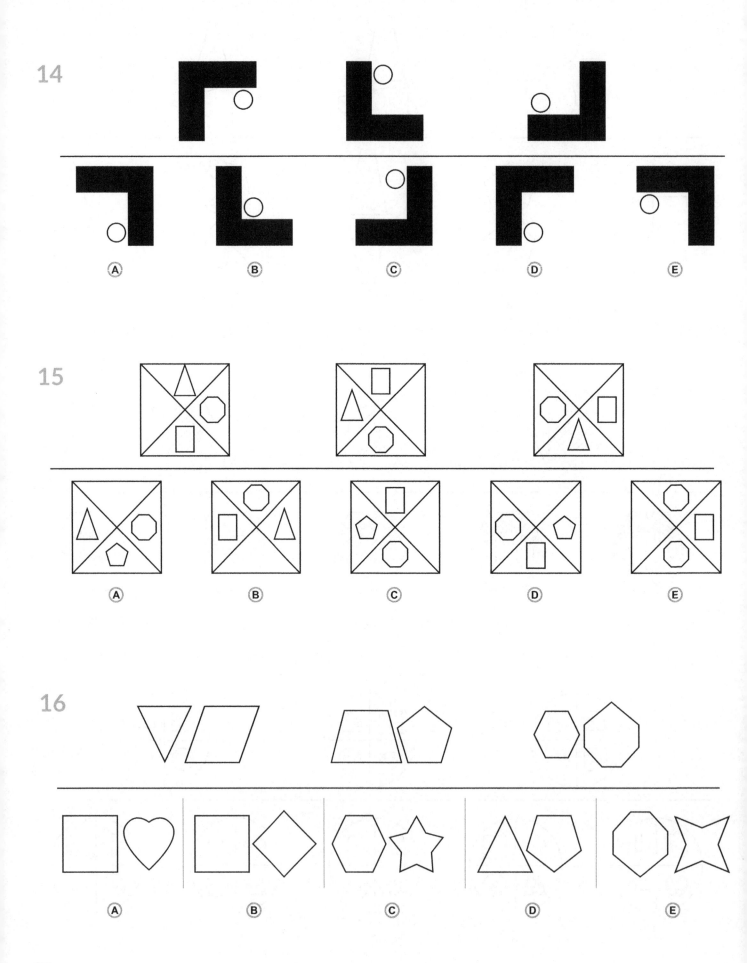

17

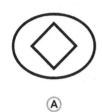    

Ⓐ Ⓑ Ⓒ Ⓓ Ⓔ

18

Ⓐ Ⓑ Ⓒ Ⓓ Ⓔ

19

Ⓐ Ⓑ Ⓒ Ⓓ Ⓔ

20

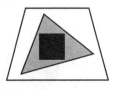  

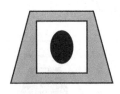 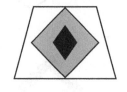 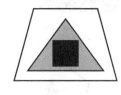 

Ⓐ Ⓑ Ⓒ Ⓓ Ⓔ

21

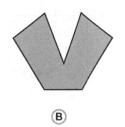   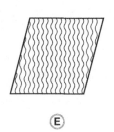

Ⓐ Ⓑ Ⓒ Ⓓ Ⓔ

22

 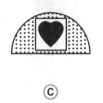  

Ⓐ Ⓑ Ⓒ Ⓓ Ⓔ

FIGURE ANALOGIES

Directions (read to child): The pictures in the top boxes go together in some way. Look at the bottom boxes. One box is empty. Look at the row of pictures next to the boxes. These are the answer choices. Which one of these choices goes with the picture in the bottom box like the pictures in the top boxes go together?

Explanation (for parents): A more detailed explanation and a Figure Analogies example question is on p. 9. If you have not already, look over p.9 (later). Following is an excerpt. As with Figure Classification, try to define a "rule" to describe how the top set belongs together. With Figure Analogies, however, make your "rule" describe a "change" that occurs from the top left box to the top right box. Next, take this "rule" describing the change, and apply it to the bottom picture. Then, look at the answer choices to determine which one would make the bottom set also follow your "rule."

Example (read to child): Let's look at the picture top picture on the left side. We see two gray arrows facing up. Look at the picture on the top right side. How has the picture changed from the original picture? We still see two gray arrows, but they have rotated. They have rotated 90 degrees clockwise. Lets try this as our rule, "rotates 90 degrees clockwise."

Now, let's look at the picture on the bottom left. Again, there are two gray arrows. If this picture rotates 90 degrees clockwise, how would it look? It would look like choice D. Choice D is the answer.

1

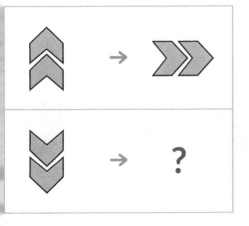         

(A)   (B)   (C)   (D)   (E)

2

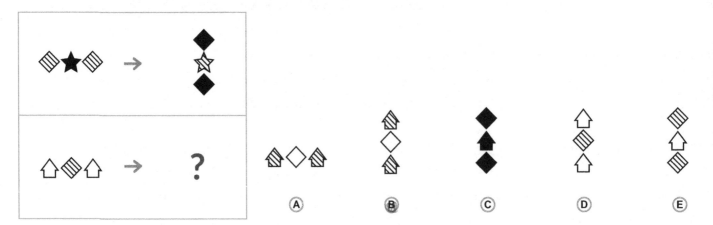

3

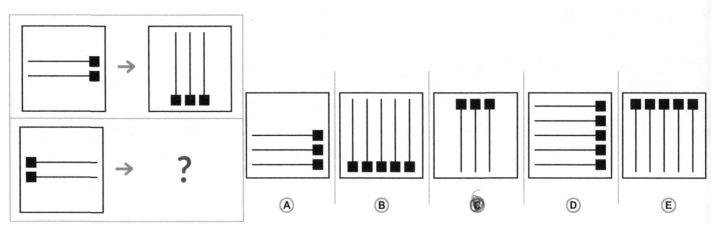

4

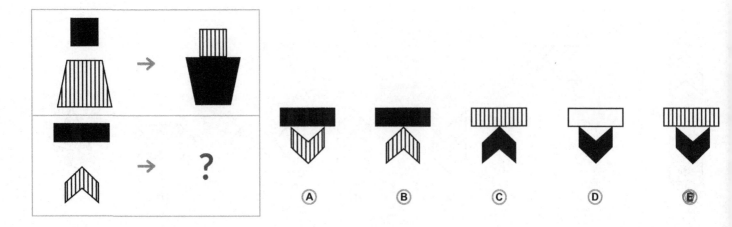

5

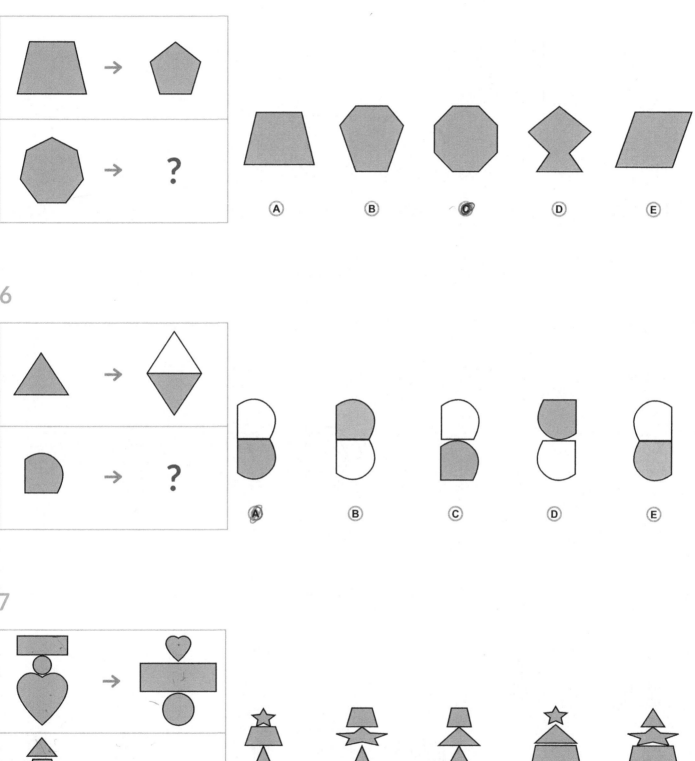

6

7

8

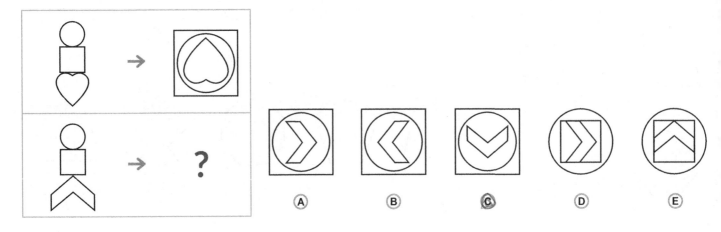

A B C D E

9

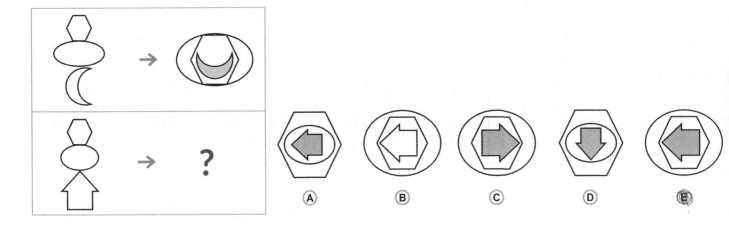

A B C D E

10

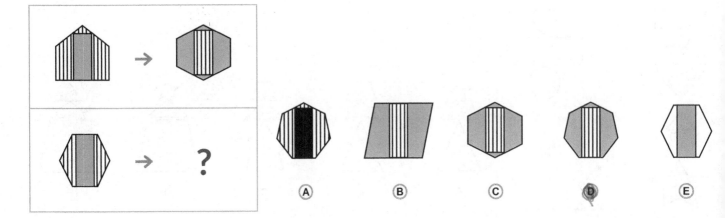

A B C D E

11

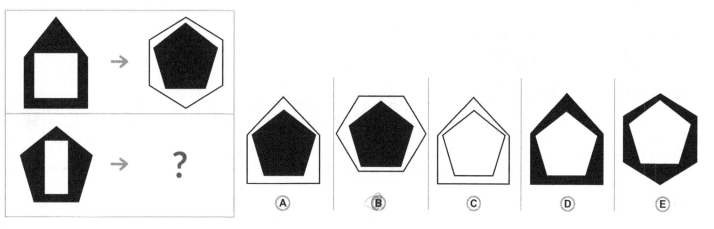

12

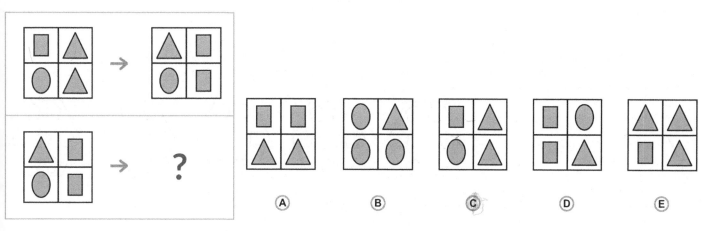

13

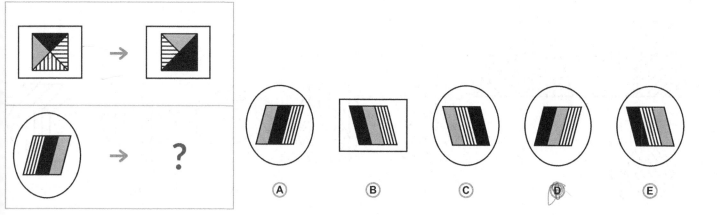

14

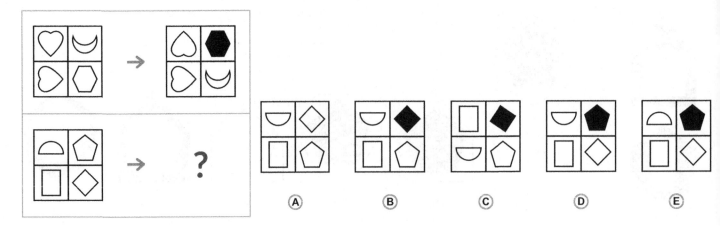

15

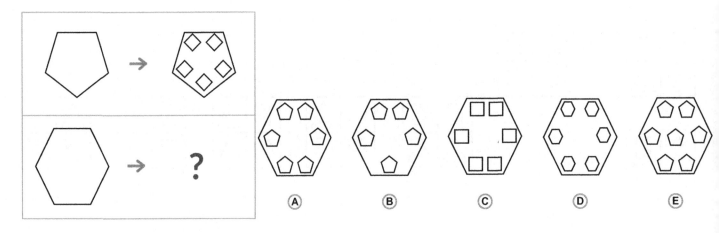

16

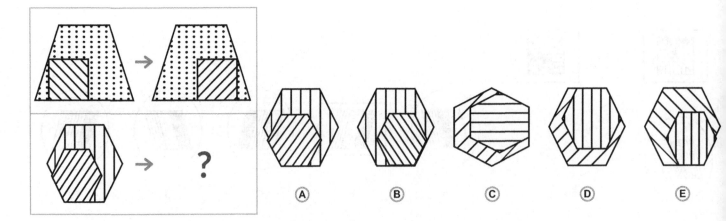

17

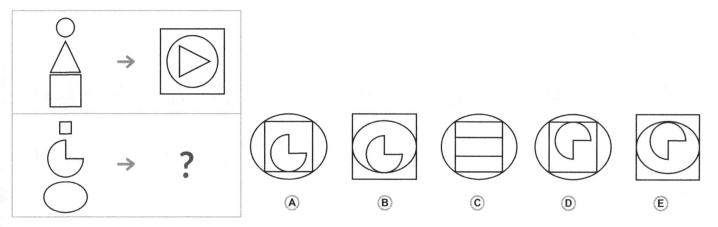

18

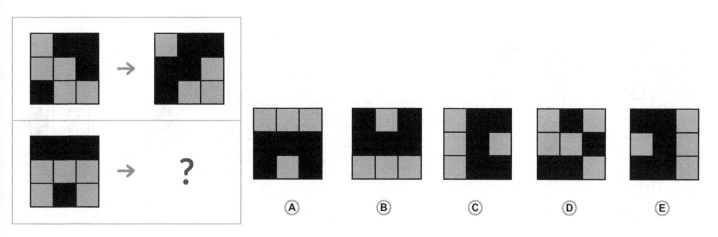

19

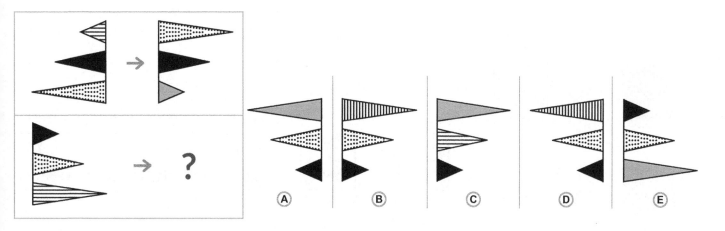

20

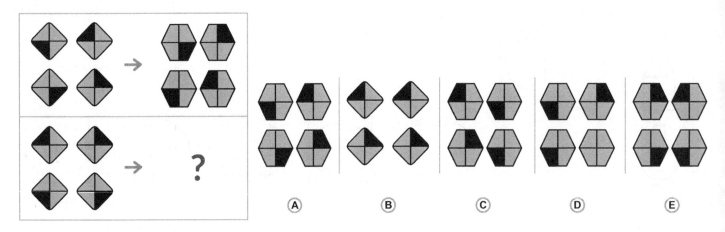

21

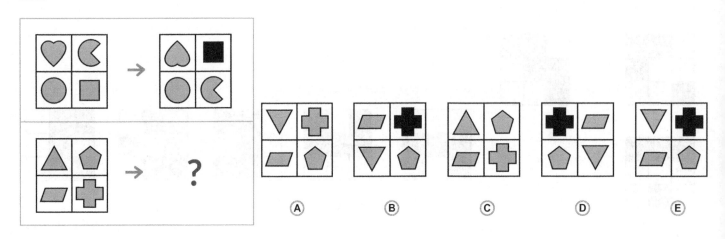

22

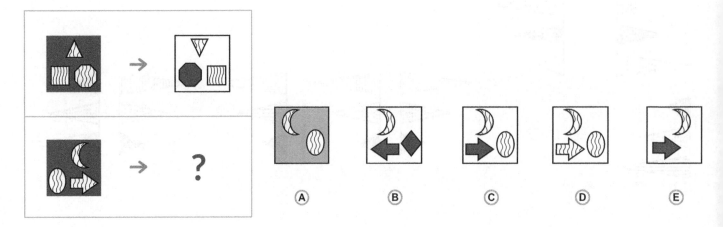

PAPER FOLDING

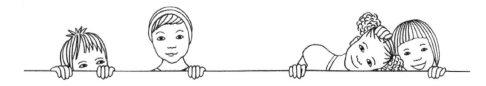

Directions (read to child): The top row of pictures shows a sheet of paper. The paper was folded, then something was cut out. Which picture in the bottom row shows how the paper would look after its unfolded?

Additional information (for parents): Starting with #6, note that some questions show paper that has been folded twice. As explained earlier in the Introduction on p. 10, it is common for children to initially be "stumped" by Paper Folding. If your child needs help, then try demonstrating with real paper. Be sure to point out the number of holes (or other shapes) made and their position after opening the paper.

1

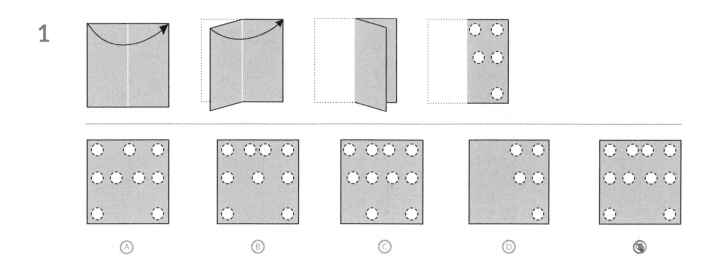

2

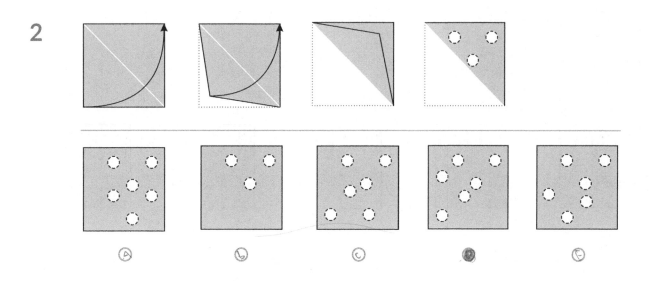

3

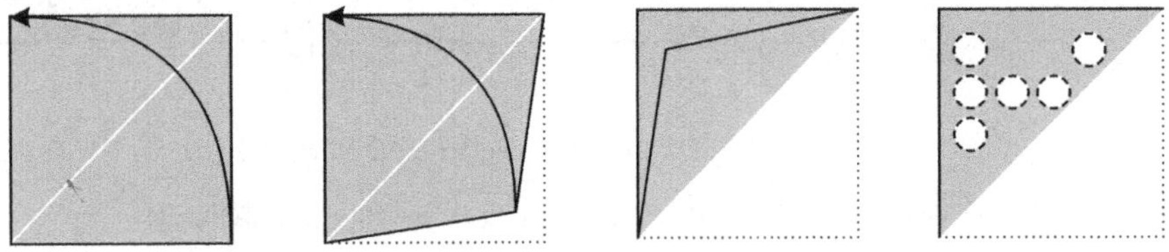

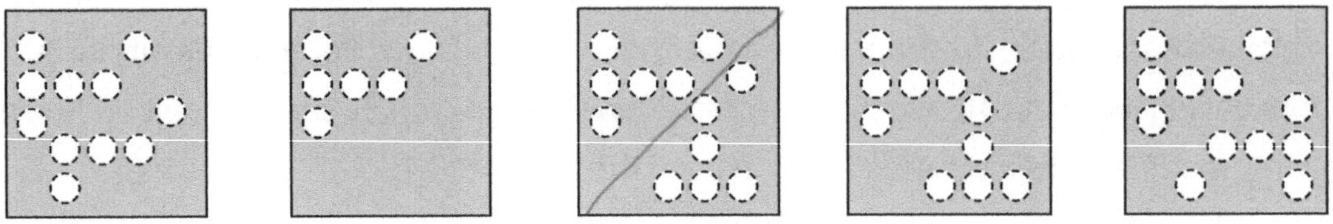

A   B   C   D   E

4

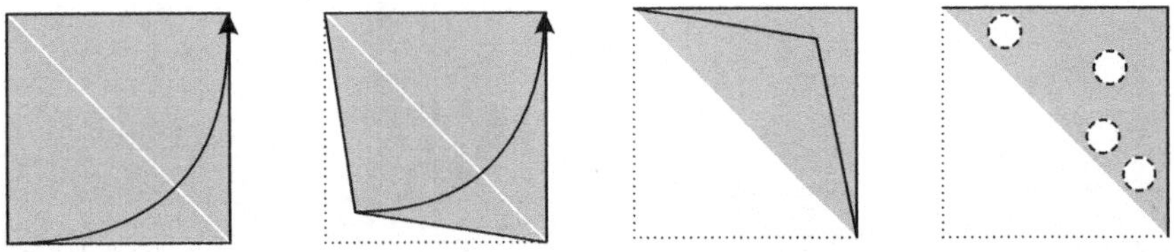

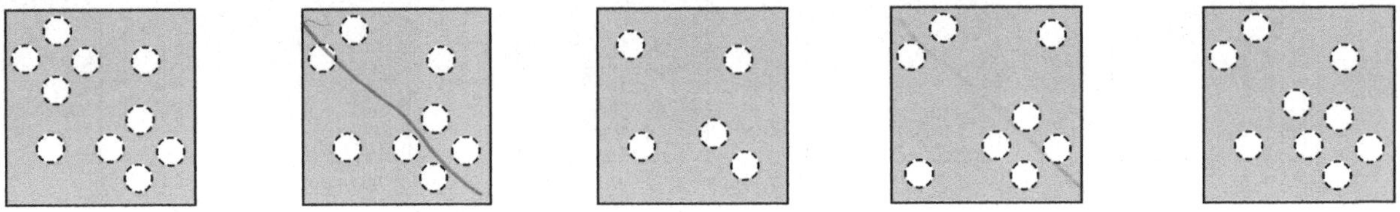

A   B   C   D   E

5

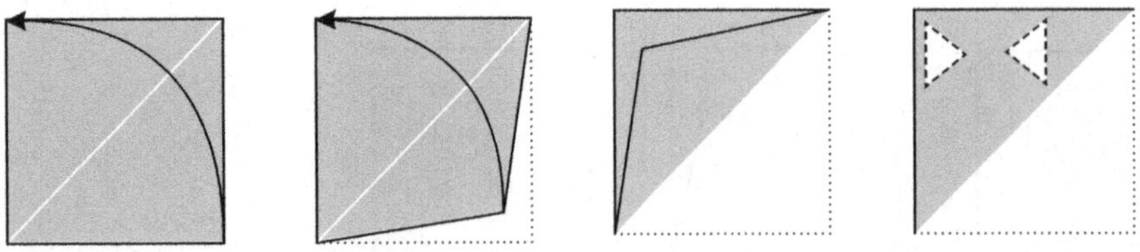

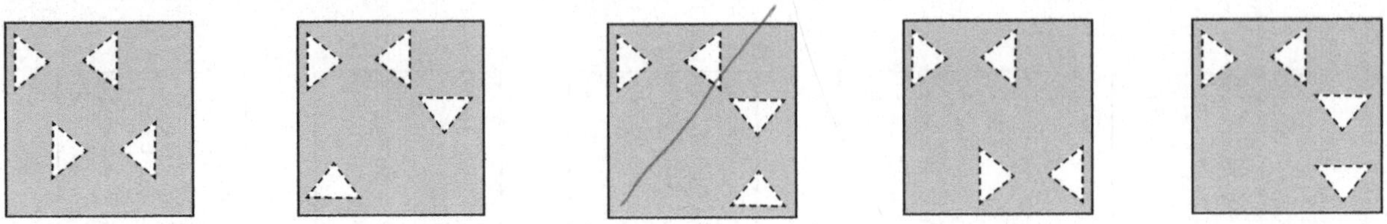

A   B   C   D   E

6

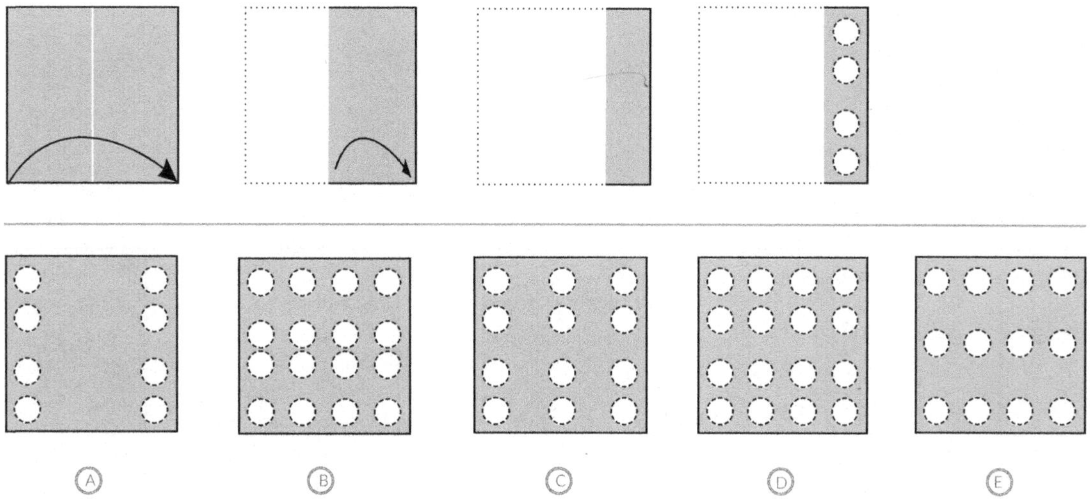

- (A)
- (B)
- (C)
- (D)
- (E)

7

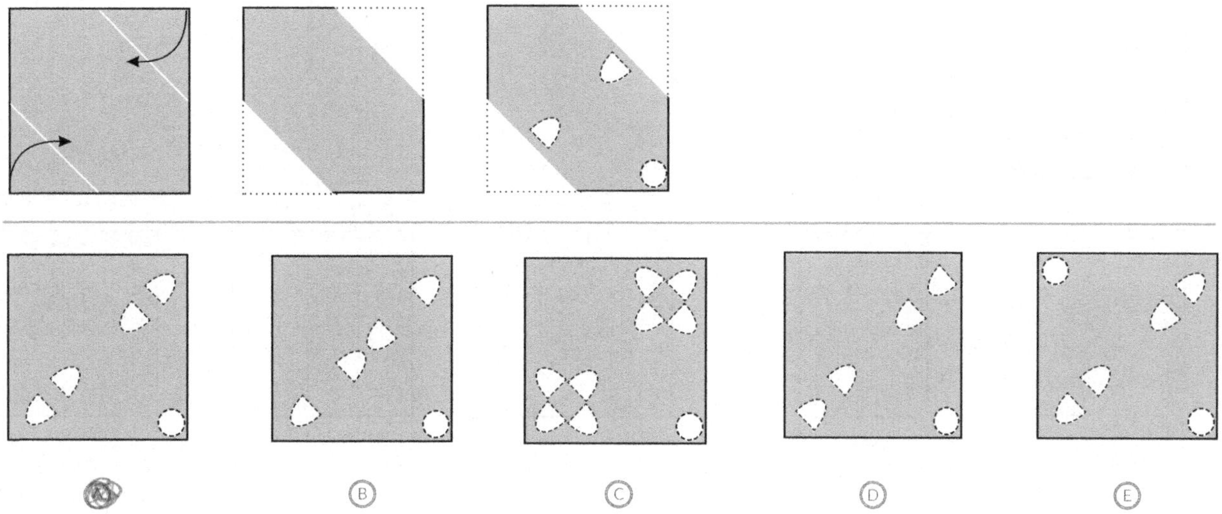

- (A)
- (B)
- (C)
- (D)
- (E)

8

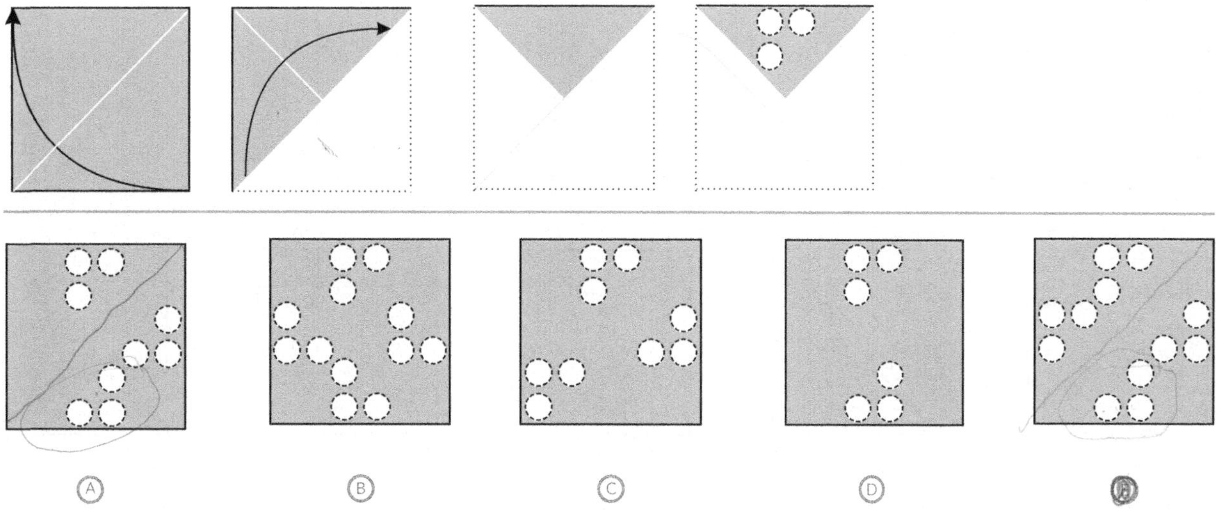

- (A)
- (B)
- (C)
- (D)
- (E)

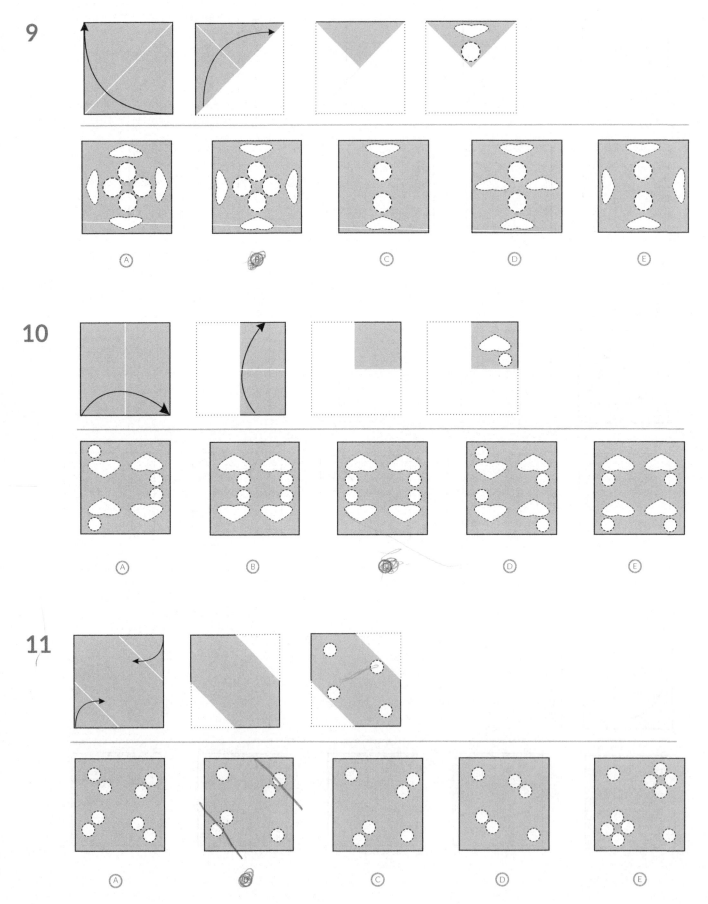

9

A   B   C   D   E

10

A   B   C   D   E

11

A   B   C   D   E

12

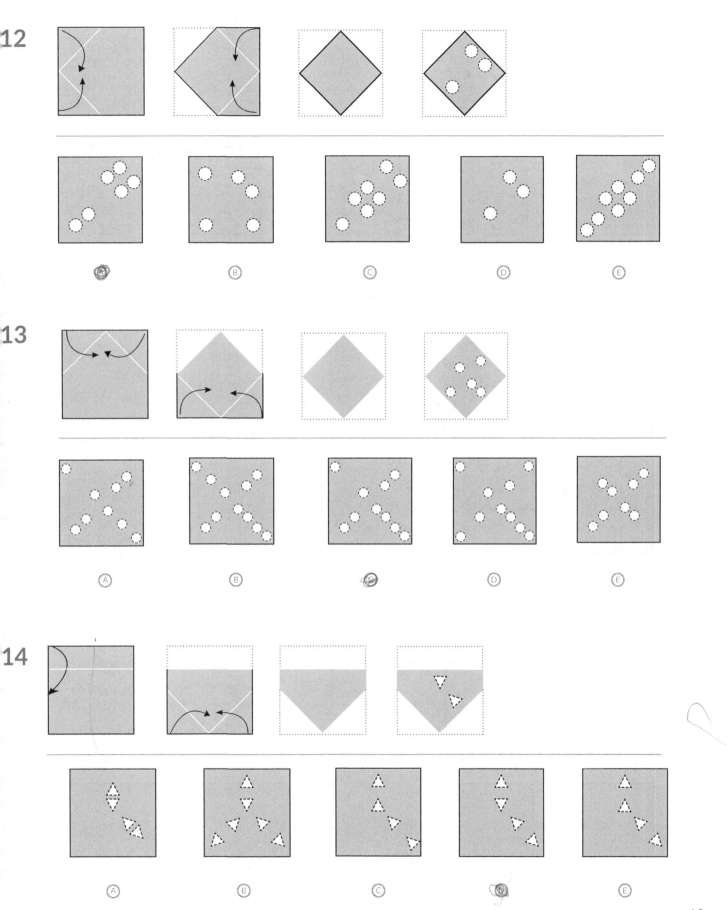

43

15

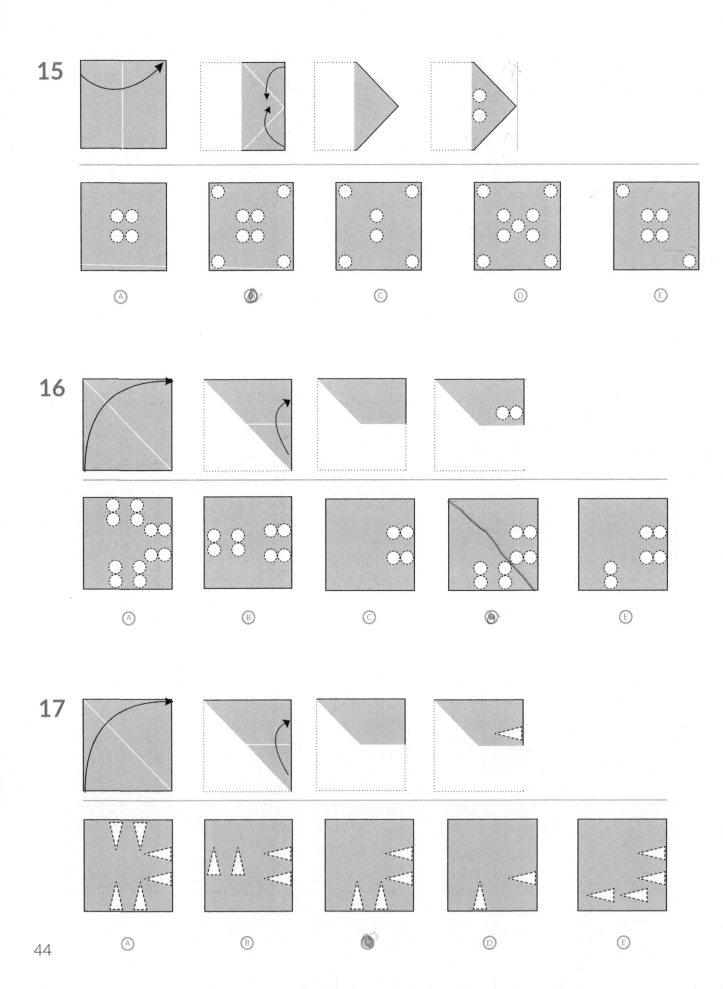

A B C D E

16

A B C D E

17

A B C D E

44

NUMBER PUZZLES

Directions (read to child):

Look at the box that has the question mark. Which number would go here so that both of the sides of this equal sign (point to the equal sign) have the same amount?

Additional information (for parents):

Be sure your child pays attention to the plus and minus signs. Some questions have two different signs. During the actual test, your child will most likely be able to use scratch paper. So, allow them to use scratch paper here if they wish. Page 11 has additional Number Puzzles tips.

Example:

The left side of the equal sign has 96. Which answer choice do you need to put in place of the question mark so that the right side of the equal sign totals 96? Twelve times what equals 96? Twelve times eight does. So, A is the correct answer.

1

| 96 = 12 x ? |

○ 8   ○ 9   ○ 84   ○ 96   ○ 108

2

| ? + ◆ = 87 |
| ◆ = 29 |

○ 3   ○ 58   ○ 116   ○ 4   ○ 29

3

$$14 \quad = \quad 98 \quad \div \quad \boxed{?}$$

○ 8   ○ 84   ⊘ 7   ○ 112   ○ 14

4

$$81 \quad - \quad 49 \quad = \quad 160 \quad \div \quad \boxed{?}$$

○ 128   ○ 6   ● 5   ○ 32   ○ 30

5

$$\boxed{?} \quad \times \quad 3 \quad = \quad 12 \quad \times \quad 7$$

○ 84   ○ 81   ○ 26   ● 28   ○ 16

28
3⟌84
6 ✓
24 ✓
24 ✓

6

$$15 \quad \times \quad 5 \quad = \quad 150 \quad \div \quad \boxed{?}$$

○ 25   ○ 15   ○ 75   ○ 20   ● 2

7

$$27 \quad \times \quad 4 \quad = \quad 89 \quad + \quad \boxed{?}$$

○ 58   ● 19   ○ 9   ○ 108   ○ 42

8

$$48 \div 3 = \boxed{?} \div 9$$

○ 144   ○ 16   ○ 45   ○ 25   ○ 5

9

$$19 \times 4 = \boxed{?} - 79$$

○ 165   ○ 145   ○ 102   ○ 155   ○ 76

10

$$\blacklozenge \times \boxed{?} = 135$$
$$\blacklozenge = 9$$

○ 126   ○ 15   ○ 135   ○ 16   ○ 17

11

$$98 \div \boxed{?} = \blacklozenge$$
$$8 \times \blacklozenge = 112$$

○ 12   ○ 8   ○ 84   ○ 14   ○ 7

12

$$78 \div \boxed{?} = \blacklozenge$$
$$98 - \blacklozenge = 72$$

○ 3   ○ 7   ○ 6   ○ 52   ○ 26

13

$? = \blacklozenge + 56$

$20 = \blacklozenge - \bullet$

$\bullet = 8$

○ 8   ○ 20   ○ 56   ○ 84   ○ 68

14

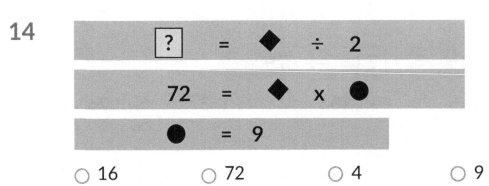

$? = \blacklozenge \div 2$

$72 = \blacklozenge \times \bullet$

$\bullet = 9$

○ 16   ○ 72   ○ 4   ○ 9   ○ 8

15

$57 - ? = 8 \times \blacklozenge$

$12 - \blacklozenge = 6$

○ 48   ○ 43   ○ 12   ○ 6   ○ 9

16

$76 \div ? = \blacklozenge$

$15 + \blacklozenge = 53$

○ 2   ○ 38   ○ 36   ○ 4   ○ 76

17

$? = \blacklozenge \times 15$

$48 = \blacklozenge \times \bullet$

$\bullet = 24$

○ 24   ○ 30   ○ 17   ○ 26   ○ 28

NUMBER ANALOGIES

Directions (read to child):
Look at the first two sets of numbers. Try to come up with a rule that both of these sets of numbers follow. Take this rule and try to figure out which answer choice goes in the place of the question mark to complete the third set of numbers.

Parent note:
A more detailed explanation and a Number Analogies example question is on p. 11. If you have not already, look over p.11 (later).

Example:
In the first set of numbers we see 67 and 49. In the second set, we see 74 and 56. How would you get from 67 to 49? How would you get from 74 to 56? In each, you subtract 18 from the first number. This could be the "rule" that both sets follow. Let's take this rule and apply it to the last set. What is the answer when you subtract 18 from 42? The answer is 24.

1   [67 → 49]   [74 → 56]   [42 → ?]

○ 34   ○ 26   ◉ 24   ○ 60   ○ 18

2   [11 → 33]   [48 → 70]   [29 → ?]

○ 61   ○ 7   ○ 22   ○ 41   ◉ 51

3   [1 → 9]   [12 → 108]   [9 → ?]

○ 18   ○ 11   ◉ 81   ○ 99   ○ 11

4   [72 → 9]   [96 → 12]   [48 → ?]

○ 16   ○ 8   ○ 56   ○ 6   ○ 40

5   [11 → 5 ½]   [20 → 10]   [15 → ?]

○ 7 ½   ○ 7   ○ 15 ½   ○ 8 ½   ○ ½

6   [4 → 16]   [6 → 36]   [7 → ?]

○ 14   ○ 49   ○ 77   ○ 37   ○ 47

7   [2/5 → 3/5]   [1/5 → 2/5]   [4/5 → ?]

○ 1/5   ○ 6/5   ○ 2/5   ○ 1   ○ 3/5

8   [0.9 → 0.09]   [0.8 → 0.08]   [2 → ?]

○ 20.2   ○ 0.02   ○ 20.0   ○ 2.0   ○ 0.2

9   [99 → 9]   [11 → 1]   [143 → ?]

○ 11   ○ 14   ○ 13   ○ 132   ○ 12

10   [6/10 → 3/5]   [5/20 → 1/4]   [6/3 → ?]

○ 6   ○ 1/3   ○ 1/2   ○ 3   ○ 2

11   [14 → 28]   [50 → 64]   [79 → ?]

○ 77   ○ 92   ○ 94   ○ 65   ○ 93

12   [48 → 80]   [80 → 112]   [59 → ?]

○ 72   ○ 82   ○ 91   ○ 92   ○ 32

13   [78 → 6]   [26 → 2]   [91 → ?]

○ 78   ● 7   ○ 104   ○ 13   ○ 19

14 [3 → 7] [5 → 11] [4 → ?]

○ 43 ○ 7 ○ 17 ○ 9 ○ 8

15 [10 → 19] [4 → 7] [8 → ?]

○ 14 ○ 17 ○ 16 ○ 15 ○ 9

16 [4 → 11] [5 → 14] [2 → ?]

○ 5 ○ 2 ○ 4 ○ 6 ○ 7

17 [2 → 9] [10 → 41] [5 → ?]

○ 20 ○ 26 ○ 2 ○ 10 ○ 21

18 [36 → 50] [14 → 28] [78 → ?]

○ 39 ○ 92 ○ 14 ○ 82 ○ 20

19   [20 → 11]   [8 → 5]   [12 → ?]

    ○ 6   ○ 3   ○ 7   ○ 9   ○ 25

20   [18 → 8]   [22 → 10]   [14 → ?]

    ○ 26   ○ 27   ○ 8   ○ 6   ○ 7

21   [25 → 6]   [30 → 7]   [10 → ?]

    ○ 2   ○ 5   ○ 6   ○ 3   ○ 4

22   [12 → 3]   [27 → 8]   [33 → ?]

    ○ 10   ○ 11   ○ 65   ○ 12   ○ 9

23   [5 → 21]   [2 → 9]   [0 → ?]

    ○ 2   ○ 7   ○ 1   ○ 4   ○ 5

NUMBER SERIES

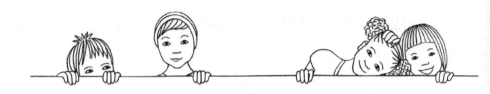

Directions (read to child):

Here, you must try to figure out a pattern that the numbers have made. Which answer choice would complete the pattern?

Example #1:

Do you see a pattern that the numbers in the series follow? What is the change between 99 and 82? You must subtract 17. We need to check that this works with the rest of the numbers. What is the change between 82 and 65? (Continue with 65 and 48 & 48 and 31.)

With each number, you subtract 17. If this is true, then what would come after 44? It's Choice A, 14.

1   **99**   **82**   **65**   **48**   **31**   **?**

    ◉ 14   ○ 24   ○ 19   ○ 30   ○ 29

2   **1**   **3**   **9**   **27**   **?**

    ○ 30   ○ 71   ○ 81   ○ 91   ○ 90

3   **41**   **40**   **38**   **37**   **35**   **34**   **32**   **?**

○ 28   ○ 29   ○ 33   ○ 31   ○ 30

4   **4.5**   **5.5**   **6.5**   **7.5**   **8.5**   **9.5**   **10.5** **?**

○ 11.0   ○ 10.6   ○ 11.5   ○ 10.55   ○ 11.6

5   **25**   **50**   **100**   **25**   **50**   **100**   **?**

○ 50   ○ 25   ○ 100   ○ 125   ○ 150

6   **91**   **90**   **88**   **87**   **85**   **84**   **82**   **?**

○ 78   ○ 79   ○ 83   ○ 81   ○ 80

7   **19**   **52**   **19**   **57**   **19**   **62**   **19**   **?**

○ 19   ○ 65   ○ 67   ○ 69   ○ 20

8   86   75   63   50   36   21   ?

○ 5   ○ 16   ○ 6   ○ 15   ○ 4

9   10   24   39   55   72   90   ?

○ 99   ○ 109   ○ 119   ○ 110   ○ 129

10   51   49   45   43   39   37   33   ?

○ 34   ○ 29   ○ 31   ○ 30   ○ 35

11   50   51   52   54   55   56   58   ?

○ 61   ○ 62   ○ 60   ○ 59   ○ 57

12   40   29   41   30   42   31   43   32   44   ?

○ 45   ○ 35   ○ 33   ○ 34   ○ 42

13 1 2 3 6 7 14 15 30 ?

  ○ 33   ○ 61   ○ 60   ○ 32   ○ 31

14 5 20 10 40 20 80 40 ?

  ○ 40   ○ 80   ○ 60   ○ 100   ○ 160

15 6 8 10 9 11 13 12 14 ?

  ○ 16   ○ 15   ○ 13   ○ 12   ○ 17

16 6 9 4 11 14 9 16 19 14 21 ?

  ○ 15   ○ 28   ○ 16   ○ 24   ○ 31

17 20 15 23 17 12 20 14 9 17 11 ?

  ○ 5   ○ 6   ○ 7   ○ 19   ○ 13

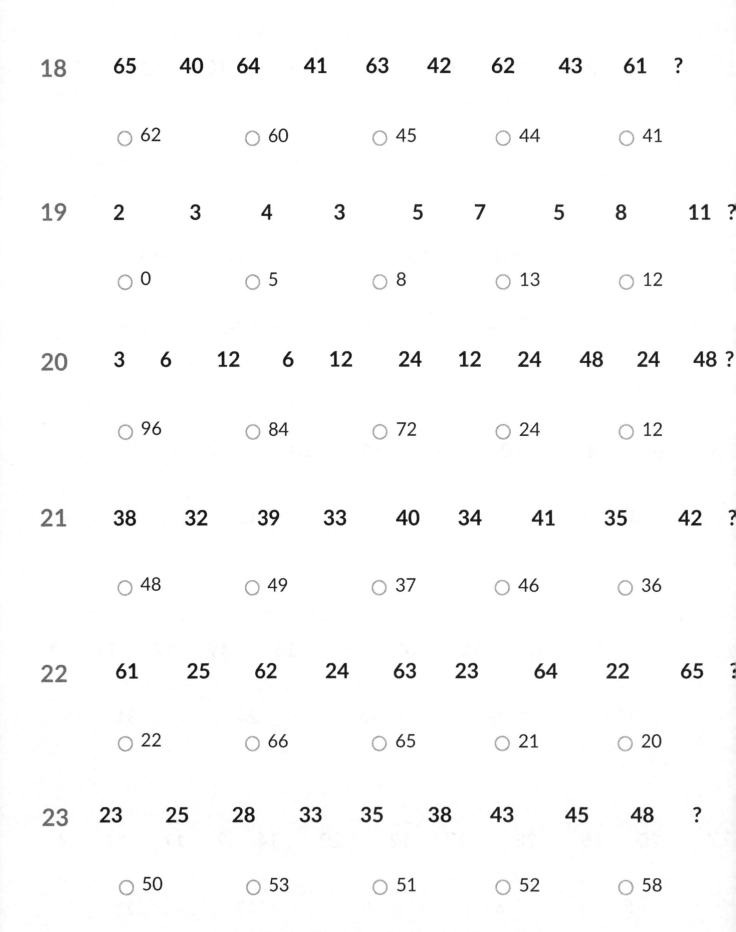

18 65 40 64 41 63 42 62 43 61 ?

○ 62   ○ 60   ○ 45   ○ 44   ○ 41

19 2 3 4 3 5 7 5 8 11 ?

○ 0   ○ 5   ○ 8   ○ 13   ○ 12

20 3 6 12 6 12 24 12 24 48 24 48 ?

○ 96   ○ 84   ○ 72   ○ 24   ○ 12

21 38 32 39 33 40 34 41 35 42 ?

○ 48   ○ 49   ○ 37   ○ 46   ○ 36

22 61 25 62 24 63 23 64 22 65 ?

○ 22   ○ 66   ○ 65   ○ 21   ○ 20

23 23 25 28 33 35 38 43 45 48 ?

○ 50   ○ 53   ○ 51   ○ 52   ○ 58

- End of Practice Test 1. Practice Test 2 begins on the next page. -

1 **Earth**   **Mars**   **Mercury**

Ⓐ planet   Ⓑ Sun   Ⓒ Neptune   Ⓓ Atlantis   Ⓔ eclipse

2 **concert**   **recital**   **play**

Ⓐ character   Ⓑ scene   Ⓒ director   Ⓓ opera   Ⓔ cinema

3 **Brazil**   **Canada**   **India**

Ⓐ Europe   Ⓑ Russia   Ⓒ Sahara   Ⓓ London   Ⓔ Central America

4 **creek**   **brook**   **river**

Ⓐ lake   Ⓑ stream   Ⓒ pond   Ⓓ swamp   Ⓔ water

5 **gradual**   **sluggish**   **unhurried**

Ⓐ slow   Ⓑ rapid   Ⓒ surprising   Ⓓ balanced   Ⓔ neutral

6 **ice maker**   **fan**   **refrigerator**

Ⓐ ice   Ⓑ oven   Ⓒ blender   Ⓓ freezer   Ⓔ water filter

7 **lime**   **lemon**   **pear**

Ⓐ cherry   Ⓑ melon   Ⓒ juice   Ⓓ grape   Ⓔ strawberry

8 **dentist**   **medic**   **pediatrician**

Ⓐ advisor   Ⓑ tutor   Ⓒ prescription   Ⓓ clinic   Ⓔ nurse

9 **captain**   **principal**   **chief**

Ⓐ counselor   Ⓑ director   Ⓒ partner   Ⓓ assistant   Ⓔ representative

10 **replica**   **clone**   **duplicate**

Ⓐ sibling   Ⓑ photo   Ⓒ model   Ⓓ copy   Ⓔ relative

11 **mix**   **merge**   **blend**

Ⓐ measure   Ⓑ enlarge   Ⓒ double   Ⓓ loosen   Ⓔ combine

12 **moss**   **mint**   **fern**

Ⓐ acorn   Ⓑ branch   Ⓒ pickle   Ⓓ pebble   Ⓔ soil

13 **reporter**   **biographer**   **playwright**

Ⓐ poet   Ⓑ play   Ⓒ doctor   Ⓓ script   Ⓔ counselor

14 **mouth**   **stomach**   **liver**

Ⓐ eyes   Ⓑ nose   Ⓒ thigh   Ⓓ heart   Ⓔ intestines

15 **newspaper**   **journal**   **magazine**

Ⓐ brochure   Ⓑ pencil   Ⓒ backpack   Ⓓ library   Ⓔ pen

16 **purse**   **suitcase**   **wallet**

Ⓐ money   Ⓑ purchase   Ⓒ mailbox   Ⓓ closet   Ⓔ bookbag

17 **enormous**   **miniature**   **colossal**

Ⓐ ratio   Ⓑ amount   Ⓒ small   Ⓓ height   Ⓔ range

18 **collect**   **gather**   **accumulate**

Ⓐ scatter   Ⓑ assemble   Ⓒ separate   Ⓓ grow   Ⓔ develop

19 **introduction**   **inauguration**   **birth**

Ⓐ invitation   Ⓑ child   Ⓒ dawn   Ⓓ section   Ⓔ conclusion

VERBAL ANALOGIES, PRACTICE TEST 2 / **Directions:** The first set of words goes together in some way. Which answer choice would make the second set of words go together in the same way as the first set?

1   **gum → wrapper : pine →**

    Ⓐ tree   Ⓑ bark   Ⓒ forest   Ⓓ pinecone   Ⓔ branch

2   **tricycle → wheel : triangle →**

    Ⓐ shape   Ⓑ triple   Ⓒ inch   Ⓓ side   Ⓔ centimeter

3   **speed → speedometer : time →**

    Ⓐ alarm   Ⓑ scale   Ⓒ clock   Ⓓ timeout   Ⓔ timetable

4   **sandpaper → rough : mirror →**

    Ⓐ smooth   Ⓑ glass   Ⓒ reflective   Ⓓ reflection   Ⓔ glass

5   **display → exhibit : hide →**

    Ⓐ protect   Ⓑ lock   Ⓒ reveal   Ⓓ seek   Ⓔ conceal

6   **build → demolish : simple →**

    Ⓐ easy   Ⓑ powerful   Ⓒ massive   Ⓓ complex   Ⓔ elegant

7   **freezer → cools : safe →**

    Ⓐ opens   Ⓑ secures   Ⓒ closes   Ⓓ alarms   Ⓔ codes

8   **shake → shook : freeze →**

    Ⓐ freezes   Ⓑ froze   Ⓒ freezing   Ⓓ freed   Ⓔ freezer

9   **wave → tsunami : building →**

    Ⓐ marina   Ⓑ cottage   Ⓒ beach   Ⓓ structure   Ⓔ skyscraper

10   **writer → poet : food →**

    Ⓐ restaurant   Ⓑ chef   Ⓒ pepper   Ⓓ water   Ⓔ plate

11   **remote → battery : dishwasher →**

    Ⓐ electricity   Ⓑ water   Ⓒ dishes   Ⓓ power   Ⓔ soap

12 today → yesterday : now →

Ⓐ later   Ⓑ again   Ⓒ previously   Ⓓ next   Ⓔ eventually

13 hoof → giraffe : paw →

Ⓐ claw   Ⓑ horse   Ⓒ zebra   Ⓓ rabbit   Ⓔ deer

14 bald → hair : dark →

Ⓐ dim   Ⓑ night   Ⓒ light   Ⓓ cloud   Ⓔ cover

15 foot → sock : planet →

Ⓐ Jupiter   Ⓑ sun   Ⓒ rocket   Ⓓ solar system   Ⓔ atmosphere

16 dim → dark : cool →

Ⓐ mild   Ⓑ frigid   Ⓒ chilled   Ⓓ hot   Ⓔ warm

17 cooperation → partner : competition →

Ⓐ opponent   Ⓑ coach   Ⓒ game   Ⓓ referee   Ⓔ assistant

18 drought → rain : hunger →

Ⓐ water   Ⓑ thirst   Ⓒ plate   Ⓓ hungry   Ⓔ food

19 telephone → communication : plane →

Ⓐ airport   Ⓑ vacation   Ⓒ travel   Ⓓ passenger   Ⓔ visiting

20 magnify → lens : cut →

Ⓐ paper   Ⓑ blade   Ⓒ point   Ⓓ sharpen   Ⓔ carving

21 small → magnifying glass : large →

Ⓐ glasses   Ⓑ lens   Ⓒ microscope   Ⓓ telescope   Ⓔ zoom

22 beaver → dam : journalist →

Ⓐ fact   Ⓑ research   Ⓒ news story   Ⓓ interview   Ⓔ reporter

1   **Anyone moving from Mexico to Canada will need to _____ to Canada's cold winter climate.**

         Ⓐ forecast   Ⓑ predict   Ⓒ encourage   Ⓓ locate   Ⓔ adapt

2   **Smoking at a gas pump is extremely dangerous, as gasoline is a _____ liquid.**

         Ⓐ clear   Ⓑ transparent   Ⓒ flammable   Ⓓ strong   Ⓔ wet

3   **In gym class we ran for 30 _____ minutes without stopping.**

         Ⓐ consecutive   Ⓑ even   Ⓒ odd   Ⓓ alternating   Ⓔ variable

4   **As spring turns into summer in the U.S., you notice that each day becomes _____ longer than the previous one.**

         Ⓐ considerably   Ⓑ slightly   Ⓒ likely   Ⓓ drastically   Ⓔ noticeably

5   **If toy store owners increase prices significantly, then the number of toys they sell will most likely _____.**

         Ⓐ rise   Ⓑ multiply   Ⓒ develop   Ⓓ plummet   Ⓔ expand

6   Driving down the mountain is a _____ journey because of the curvy roads and low visibility.

(A) compelling   (B) pleasant   (C) steep   (D) lively   (E) treacherous

7   Only an expert jeweler would notice the _____ differences between this real diamond and a fake one.

(A) obvious   (B) clear   (C) noticeable   (D) subtle   (E) expensive

8   The two enemies decided to _____ a treaty that both sides would agree to.

(A) negotiate   (B) avoid   (C) refuse   (D) reject   (E) battle

9   During metamorphosis a tadpole _____ into a frog.

(A) expands   (B) transforms   (C) shrinks   (D) enlarges   (E) inflates

10   You can only open and print this document, but if you want to _____ it in any way, you will need the password to make any changes.

(A) view   (B) read   (C) notice   (D) modify   (E) skim

11   Parents cannot serve as referees for their children's sports competitions because often the parents would not be _____.

(A) active   (B) energetic   (C) interested   (D) involved   (E) impartial

12   The islands are _____ - a ten hour plane ride is required to reach their airport.

(A) remote   (B) uninhabited   (C) convenient   (D) contiguous   (E) abandoned

13   The more _____ a place has, the more homes are required.

(A) tourists   (B) inhabitants   (C) dwellings   (D) vegetation   (E) owners

14   Because the jungle was so _____, we could hardly walk through it.

(A) tropical   (B) towering   (C) dense   (D) heavy   (E) sparse

15   Because the judge showed _____toward one side in the trial, she is no longer allowed to serve as a judge.

(A) bias   (B) rules   (C) regulations   (D) evidence   (E) laws

16 If each of us _____ at least $5, together we will have enough to purchase a gift for our teacher.

(A) receives (B) contributes (C) considers (D) retains (E) deducts

17 To ensure sufficient space for the _____ shipments, load them onto the plane first.

(A) heavy (B) distant (C) priority (D) minuscule (E) irrelevant

18 As the empire expands, it continues to look for more land to _____.

(A) evacuate (B) diminish (C) surrender (D) acquire (E) release

19 After close examination, the art dealer determined the painting was an _____ one, created by a famous artist and worth a fortune.

(A) authentic (B) interesting (C) imitation (D) eye-catching (E) enormous

20 In general, writers use bold font for words or ideas they want to _____.

(A) overlook (B) summarize (C) pronounce (D) ignore (E) emphasize

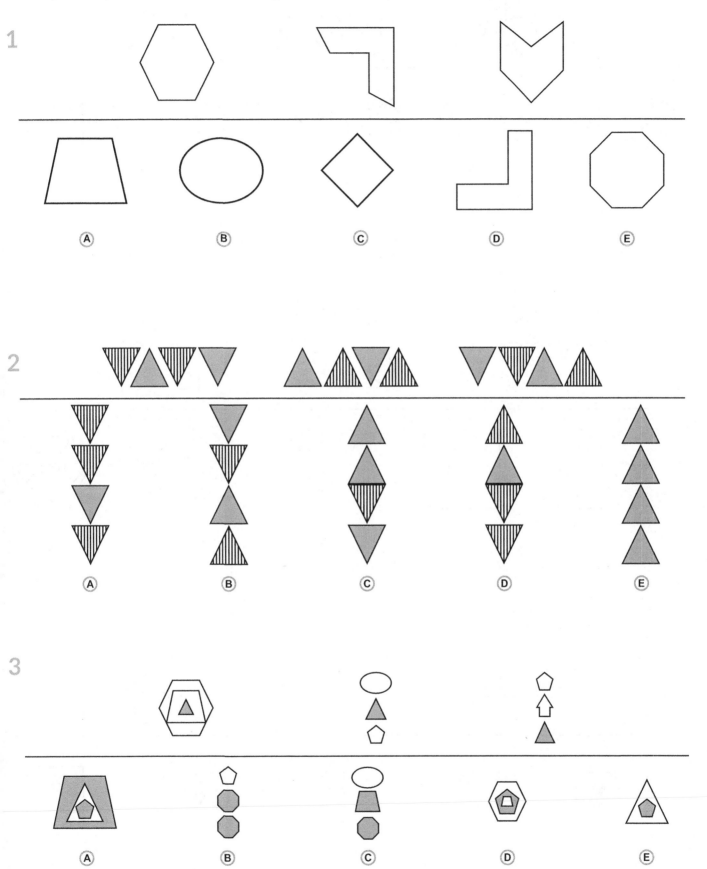

4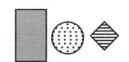

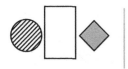 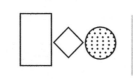 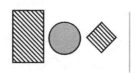 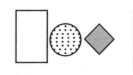 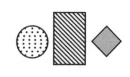

Ⓐ   Ⓑ   Ⓒ   Ⓓ   Ⓔ

5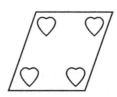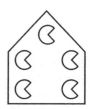

Ⓐ   Ⓑ   Ⓒ   Ⓓ   Ⓔ

6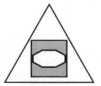

 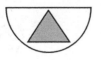

Ⓐ   Ⓑ   Ⓒ   Ⓓ   Ⓔ

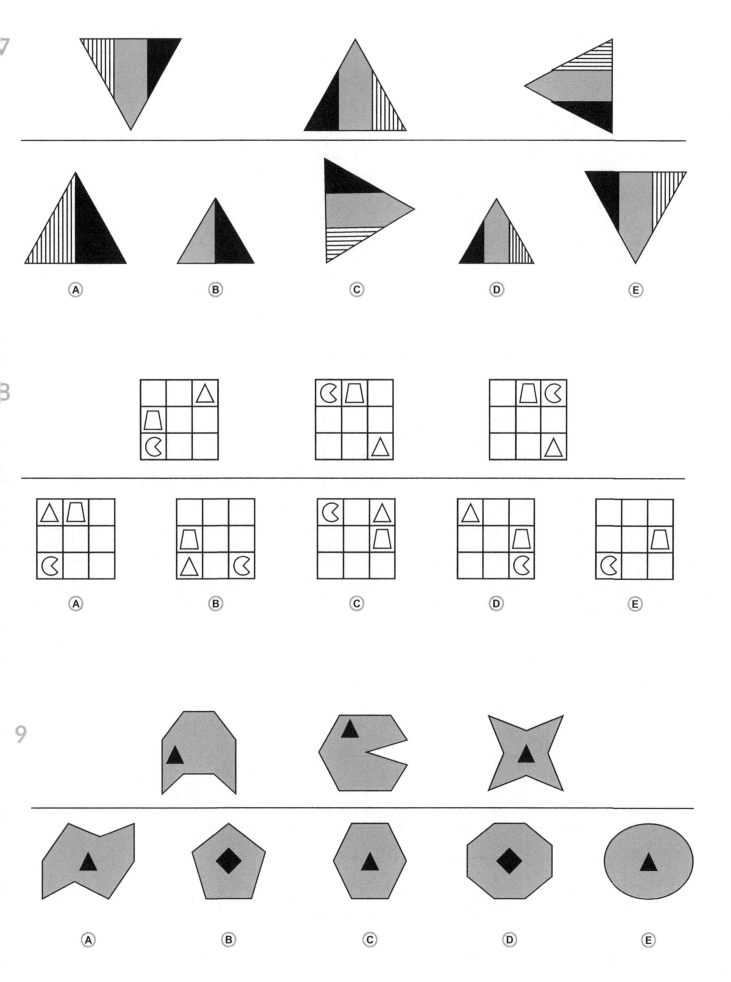

10

  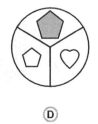 

(A) (B) (C) (D) (E)

11

 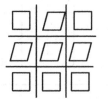 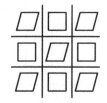

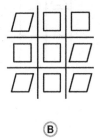 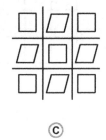 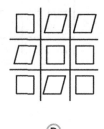 

(A) (B) (C) (D) (E)

12

    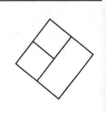

(A) (B) (C) (D) (E)

13

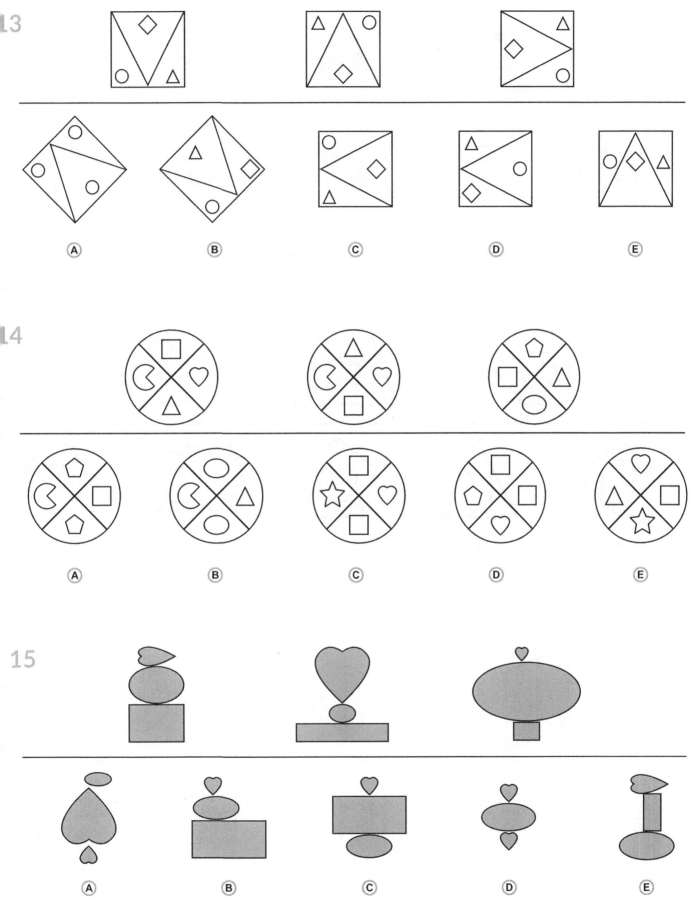

14

15

16

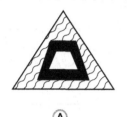 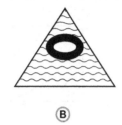 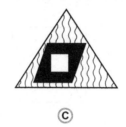 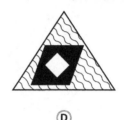 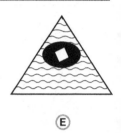

Ⓐ Ⓑ Ⓒ Ⓓ Ⓔ

17

 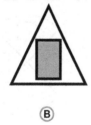 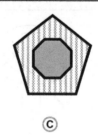 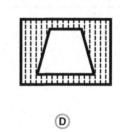 

Ⓐ Ⓑ Ⓒ Ⓓ Ⓔ

18

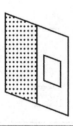

Ⓐ Ⓑ Ⓒ Ⓓ Ⓔ

19

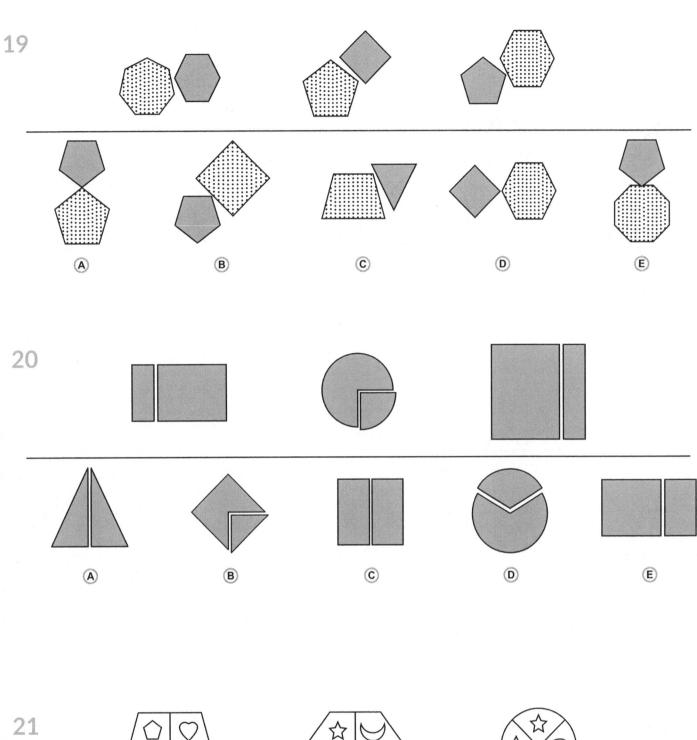

20

21

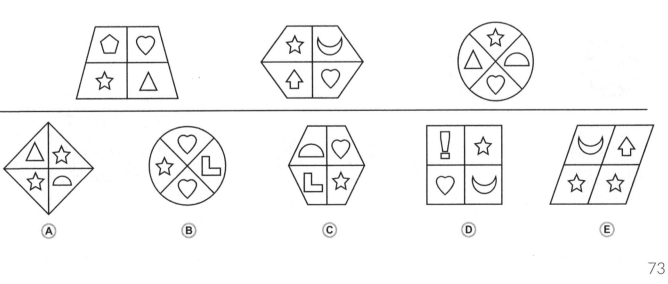

1

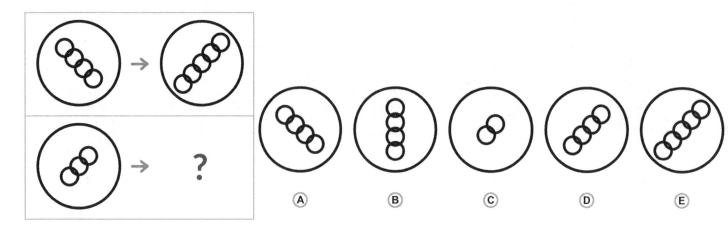

2

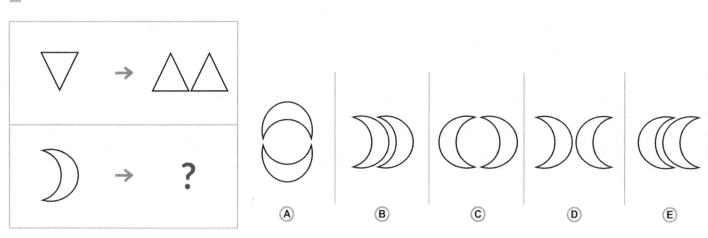

3

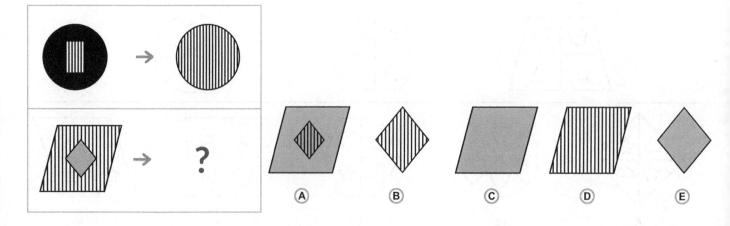

4

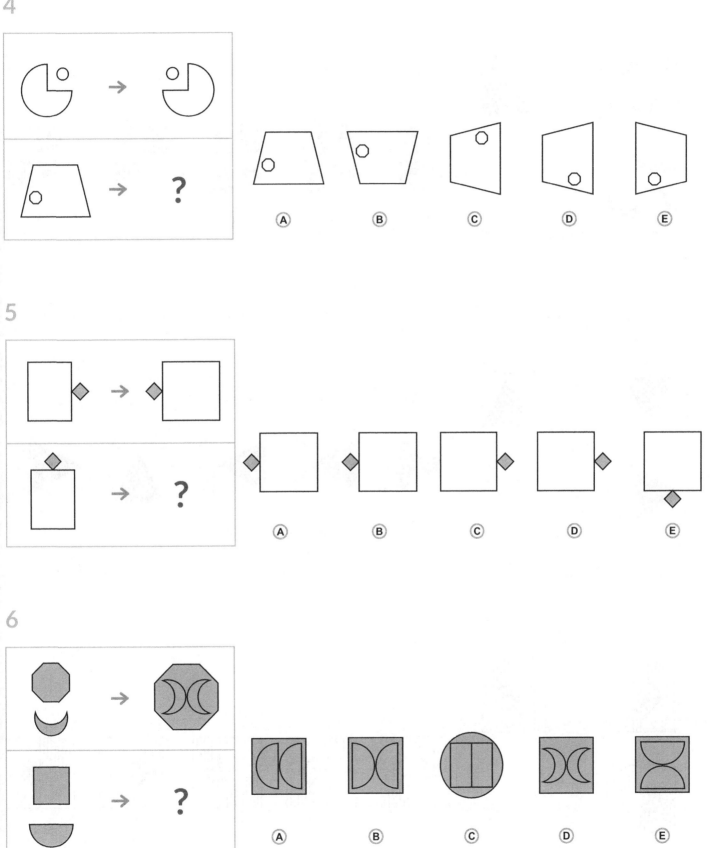

5

6

7

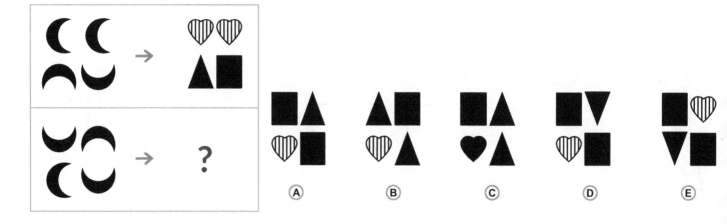

8

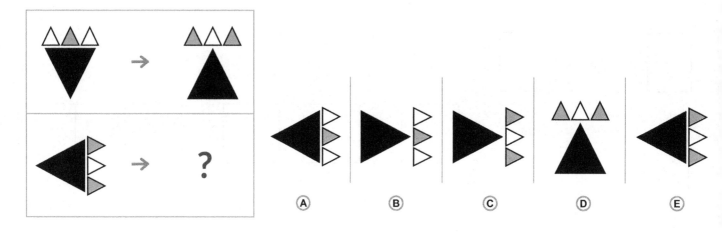

9

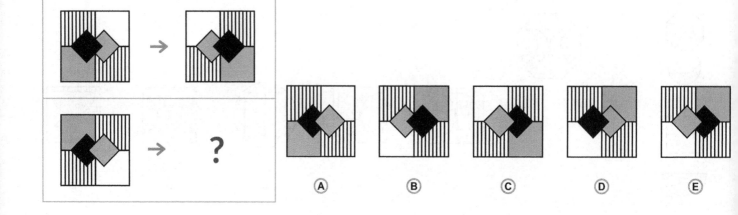

10

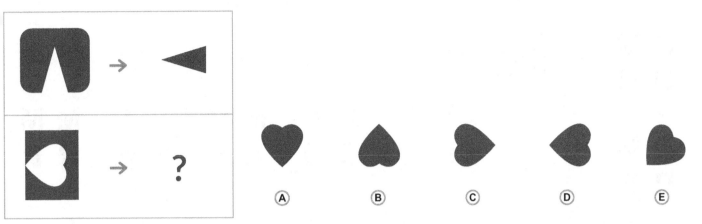

11

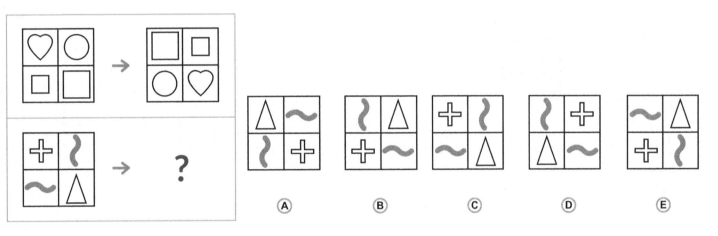

12

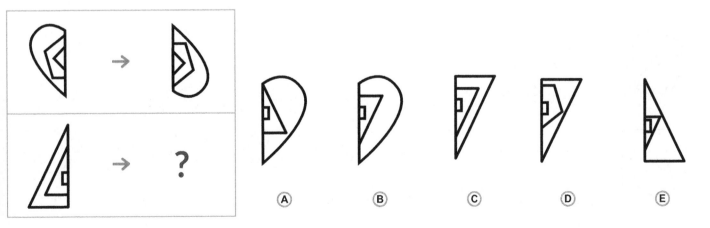

13

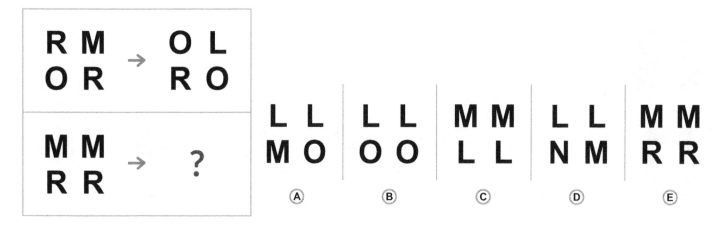

14

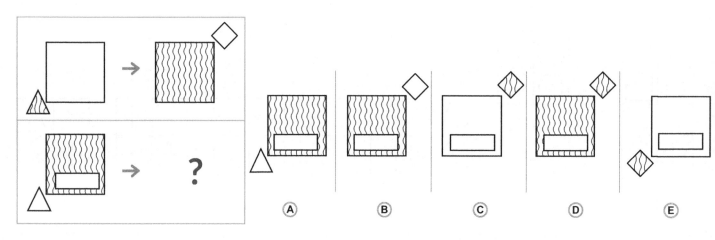

15

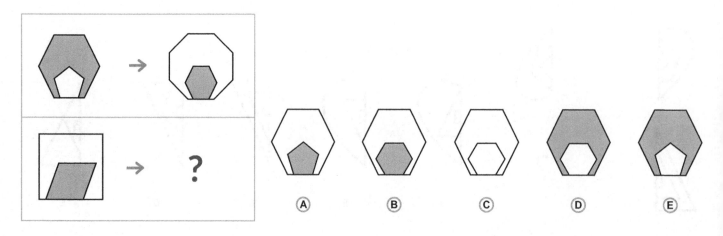

16

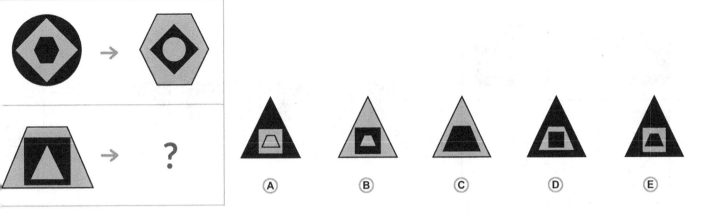

17

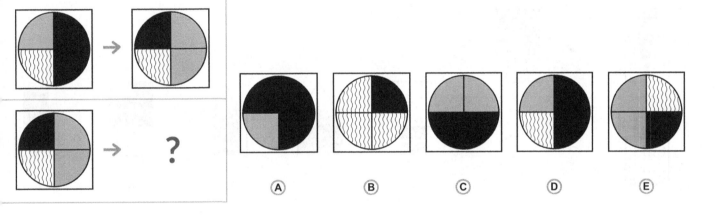

18

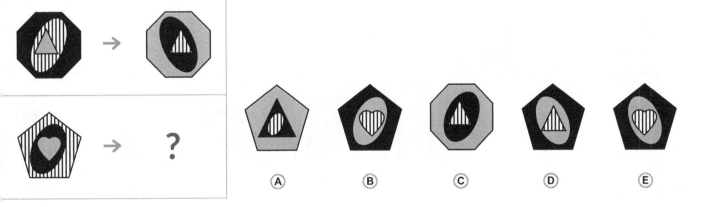

19

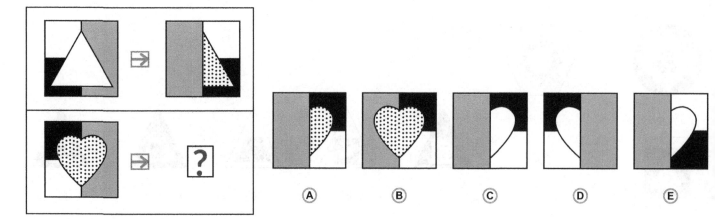

20

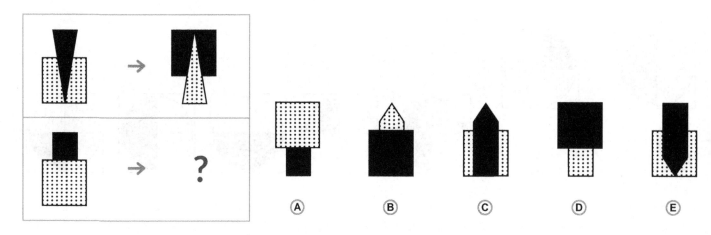

21

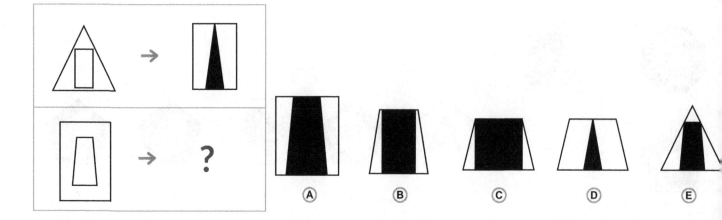

80

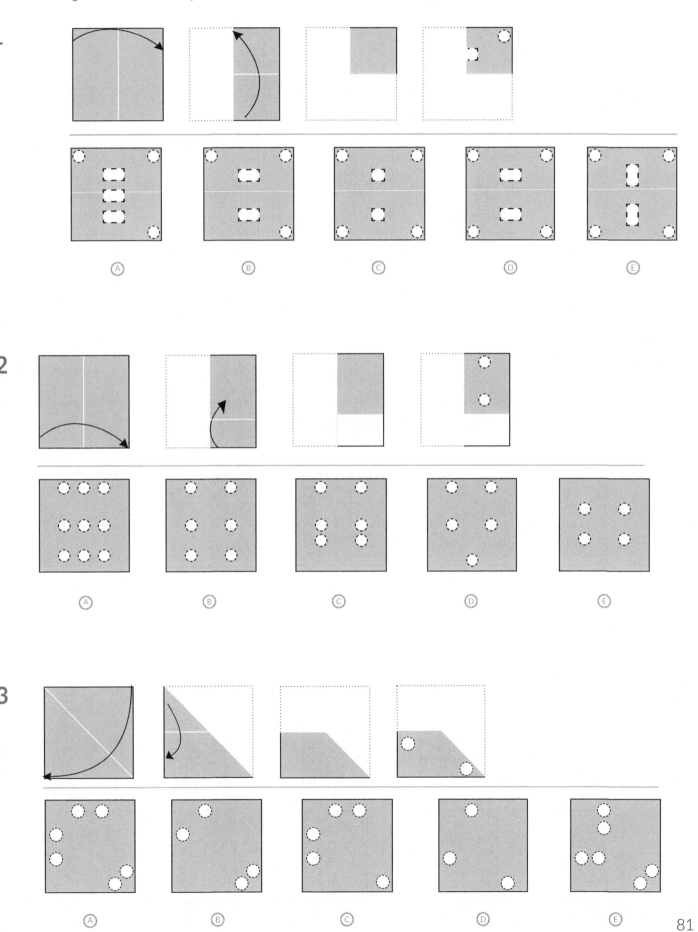

81

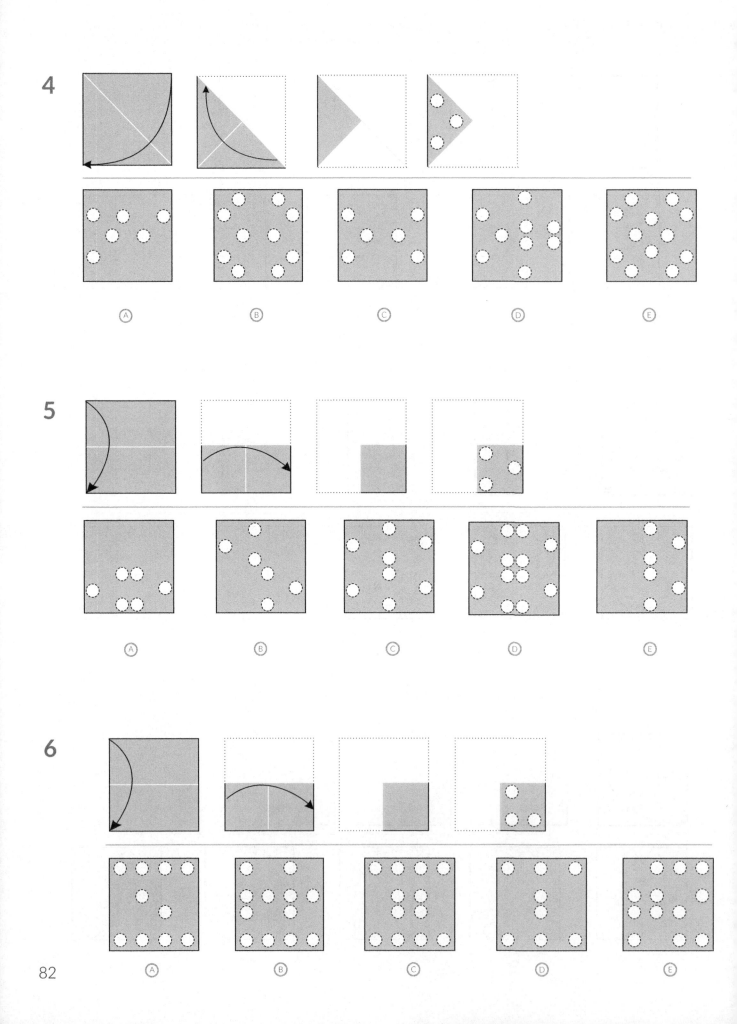

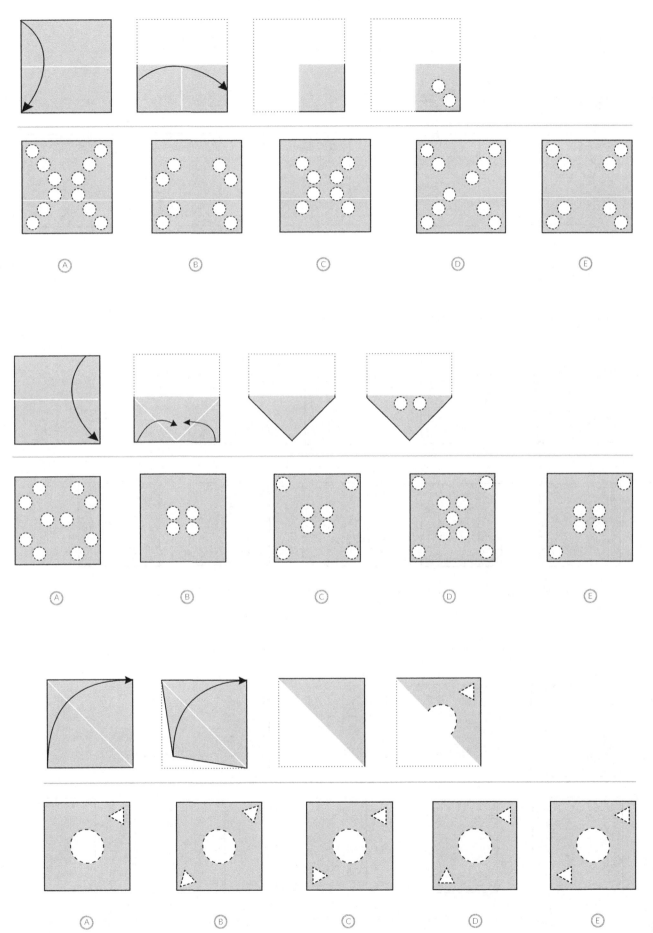

10

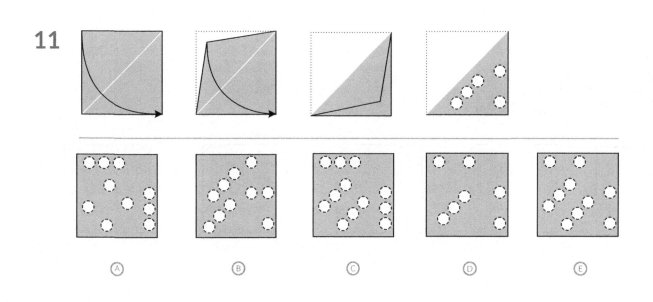

11

12

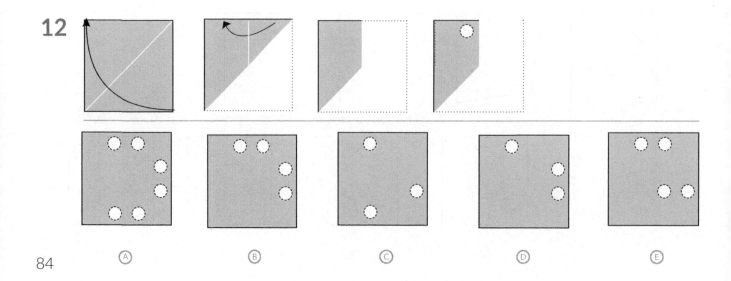

13

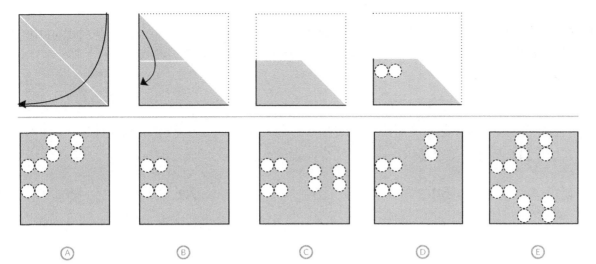

    Ⓐ   Ⓑ   Ⓒ   Ⓓ   Ⓔ

14

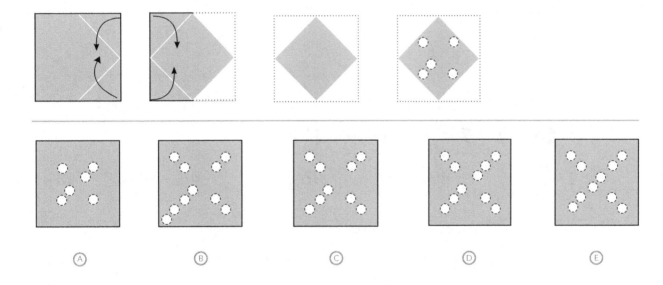

    Ⓐ   Ⓑ   Ⓒ   Ⓓ   Ⓔ

15

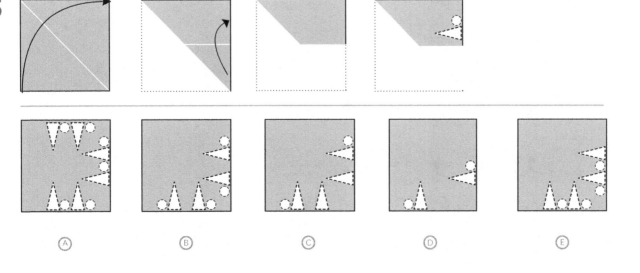

    Ⓐ   Ⓑ   Ⓒ   Ⓓ   Ⓔ

NUMBER PUZZLES, PRACTICE TEST 2 / Directions: What answer choice should you put in the place of the question mark so that both sides of the equal sign total the same amount?

1

$18 = 72 \div \boxed{?}$

Ⓐ 4 Ⓑ 54 Ⓒ 6 Ⓓ 90 Ⓔ 6

2

$13 \times 6 = 90 - \boxed{?}$

Ⓐ 65 Ⓑ 11 Ⓒ 3 Ⓓ 71 Ⓔ 12

3

$14 \times 7 = 2 \times \boxed{?}$

Ⓐ 1 Ⓑ 49 Ⓒ 96 Ⓓ 44 Ⓔ 48

4

$42 + 38 = 20 + \boxed{?}$

Ⓐ 40 Ⓑ 80 Ⓒ 20 Ⓓ 60 Ⓔ 4

5

$54 \div \boxed{?} = \blacklozenge$

$12 \times \blacklozenge = 72$

Ⓐ 9 Ⓑ 6 Ⓒ 48 Ⓓ 7 Ⓔ 72

6 $95 - 79 = \boxed{?} \div 3$

(A) 58   (B) 48   (C) 30   (D) 79   (E) 16

7 $\boxed{?} \div 12 = 60 \div 15$

(A) 33   (B) 12   (C) 48   (D) 64   (E) 57

8 $65 + 19 - 20 = 32 \times \boxed{?}$

(A) 34   (B) 64   (C) 32   (D) 2   (E) 29

9 $51 \div \boxed{?} = \blacklozenge$

$49 + \blacklozenge = 66$

(A) 3   (B) 17   (C) 4   (D) 5   (E) 15

10 $24 \times 4 = \boxed{?} \times 12$

(A) 16   (B) 28   (C) 10   (D) 9   (E) 8

11

85 ÷ 5 = ? - 23

(A) 20   (B) 63   (C) 17   (D) 67   (E) 40

12

70 ÷ ? = ◆

64 + ◆ = 99

(A) 99   (B) 2   (C) 6   (D) 34   (E) 35

13

54 ÷ ? = ◆

30 x ◆ = 90

(A) 18   (B) 60   (C) 6   (D) 24   (E) 5

14

5 x ? = ◆

74 - ◆ = 9

(A) 60   (B) 15   (C) 13   (D) 65   (E) 75

15

32 + 19 = ? - 34

(A) 17   (B) 85   (C) 84   (D) 52   (E) 51

16

$$? = \blacklozenge + 47$$

$$30 = \blacklozenge - \bullet$$

$$\bullet = 4$$

(A) 73 (B) 71 (C) 17 (D) 81 (E) 91

17

$$? = \blacklozenge \times 9$$

$$56 = \blacklozenge \times \bullet$$

$$\bullet = 8$$

(A) 39 (B) 72 (C) 63 (D) 9 (E) 8

18

$$91 - ? = 3 \times \blacklozenge$$

$$41 - \blacklozenge = 16$$

(A) 63 (B) 91 (C) 45 (D) 16 (E) 75

19

$$93 \div ? = \blacklozenge$$

$$62 + \blacklozenge = 93$$

(A) 3 (B) 2 (C) 31 (D) 32 (E) 62

20

$$? = \blacklozenge \times 14$$

$$90 = \blacklozenge \times \bullet$$

$$\bullet = 18$$

(A) 72 (B) 70 (C) 5 (D) 6 (E) 18

NUMBER ANALOGIES, PRACTICE TEST 2 / Directions: Look at the first two sets of numbers. Come up with a rule that both sets follow. Take this rule to figure out which answer choice goes in the place of the question mark.

1   [42 → 80]   [59 → 97]   [61 → ?]

Ⓐ 109   Ⓑ 89   Ⓒ 38   Ⓓ 23   Ⓔ 99

2   [3 → 42]   [6 → 84]   [2 → ?]

Ⓐ 28   Ⓑ 14   Ⓒ 16   Ⓓ 24   Ⓔ 20

3   [120 → 10]   [12 → 1]   [60 → ?]

Ⓐ 48   Ⓑ 72   Ⓒ 5   Ⓓ 12   Ⓔ 49

4   [86 → 43]   [1 → 0.5]   [22 → ?]

Ⓐ 20   Ⓑ 2   Ⓒ 10   Ⓓ 11   Ⓔ 44

5   [2 → 4]   [1 → 1]   [7 → ?]

Ⓐ 14   Ⓑ 49   Ⓒ 77   Ⓓ 21   Ⓔ 7

6   [1 → ½]   [½ → ¼]   [50 → ?]

Ⓐ 49   Ⓑ 50.5   Ⓒ 49 ⅕   Ⓓ 50 ½   Ⓔ 25

7 [³⁄₃ → 1] [¼ → ²⁄₈] [¹⁰⁄₅ → ?]

Ⓐ 2 Ⓑ ⁵⁄₁₀ Ⓒ 50 Ⓓ 5 Ⓔ ⅕

8 [0.7 → 0.07] [0.2 → 0.02] [3 → ?]

Ⓐ 0.33 Ⓑ 0.03 Ⓒ 3.3 Ⓓ 3.0 Ⓔ 0.3

9 [50 → 5] [100 → 10] [0.6 → ?]

Ⓐ 60 Ⓑ 6 Ⓒ 0.06 Ⓓ 16 Ⓔ 6.1

10 [33 → 66] [48 → 81] [39 → ?]

Ⓐ 93 Ⓑ 62 Ⓒ 33 Ⓓ 6 Ⓔ 72

11 [2 → 5] [7 → 15] [20 → ?]

Ⓐ 23 Ⓑ 22 Ⓒ 40 Ⓓ 41 Ⓔ 31

12 [4 → 21] [10 → 51] [9 → ?]

Ⓐ 44 Ⓑ 45 Ⓒ 46 Ⓓ 71 Ⓔ 15

13   [5 → 13]   [9 → 25]   [6 → ?]

Ⓐ 18   Ⓑ 16   Ⓒ 20   Ⓓ 21   Ⓔ 17

14   [2 → 7]   [10 → 39]   [4 → ?]

Ⓐ 16   Ⓑ 9   Ⓒ 17   Ⓓ 15   Ⓔ 7

15   [32 → 6]   [52 → 26]   [30 → ?]

Ⓐ 4   Ⓑ 15   Ⓒ 56   Ⓓ 16   Ⓔ 32

16   [81 → 9]   [9 → 1]   [0 → ?]

Ⓐ 81   Ⓑ 9   Ⓒ 0   Ⓓ 19   Ⓔ 1

17   [20 → 6]   [32 → 9]   [36 → ?]

Ⓐ 33   Ⓑ 4   Ⓒ 10   Ⓓ 9   Ⓔ 8

18   [42 → 22]   [58 → 30]   [18 → ?]

Ⓐ 17   Ⓑ 12   Ⓒ 11   Ⓓ 9   Ⓔ 10

19 [⁶⁄₁₂ → ½]   [¹²⁄₄ → 3]   [9 → ?]

(A) ⁹⁄₉   (B) ²⁄₁₈   (C) 9.9   (D) 9.1   (E) ¹⁸⁄₂

20 [0.2 → 2]   [9 → 90]   [0.5 → ?]

(A) 5   (B) 0.55   (C) 5.5   (D) 50   (E) 0.05

21 [15 → 6]   [36 → 13]   [21 → ?]

(A) 5   (B) 24   (C) 6   (D) 8   (E) 7

22 [60 → 5]   [36 → 3]   [96 → ?]

(A) 6   (B) 8   (C) 84   (D) 32   (E) 9

23 [9 → 35]   [10 → 39]   [7 → ?]

(A) 28   (B) 29   (C) 10   (D) 20   (E) 27

24 [42 → 23]   [28 → 16]   [80 → ?]

(A) 40   (B) 42   (C) 38   (D) 68   (E) 61

1   9   21   33   45   57   69   ?

   Ⓐ 81   Ⓑ 71   Ⓒ 79   Ⓓ 91   Ⓔ 80

2   3   6   12   24   48   ?

   Ⓐ 86   Ⓑ 50   Ⓒ 82   Ⓓ 84   Ⓔ 96

3   8.4   10.4   12.4   14.4   16.4   ?

   Ⓐ 16.6   Ⓑ 20.4   Ⓒ 18.4   Ⓓ 18.6   Ⓔ 22.4

4   22.3   21.3   20.3   19.3   18.3   ?

   Ⓐ 17.0   Ⓑ 18.4   Ⓒ 18.2   Ⓓ 17.3   Ⓔ 18.33

5   81   81   79   79   77   77   ?

   Ⓐ 76   Ⓑ 75   Ⓒ 77   Ⓓ 73   Ⓔ 70

7   **15**   **7**   **25**   **7**   **35**   **7**   **?**

Ⓐ 45   Ⓑ 7   Ⓒ 40   Ⓓ 30   Ⓔ 17

10   **11**   **19**   **20**   **28**   **29**   **37**   **38**   **?**

Ⓐ 36   Ⓑ 46   Ⓒ 56   Ⓓ 39   Ⓔ 40

45   **43**   **38**   **36**   **31**   **29**   **24**   **22**   **?**

Ⓐ 20   Ⓑ 17   Ⓒ 27   Ⓓ 18   Ⓔ 15

80   **79**   **77**   **74**   **70**   **65**   **59**   **52**   **?**

Ⓐ 60   Ⓑ 48   Ⓒ 44   Ⓓ 46   Ⓔ 50

32   **16**   **8**   **32**   **16**   **8**   **?**

Ⓐ 32   Ⓑ 24   Ⓒ 16   Ⓓ 8   Ⓔ 4

42   **43**   **44**   **49**   **50**   **51**   **56**   **57**   **58**   **?**

Ⓐ 63   Ⓑ 59   Ⓒ 60   Ⓓ 53   Ⓔ 73

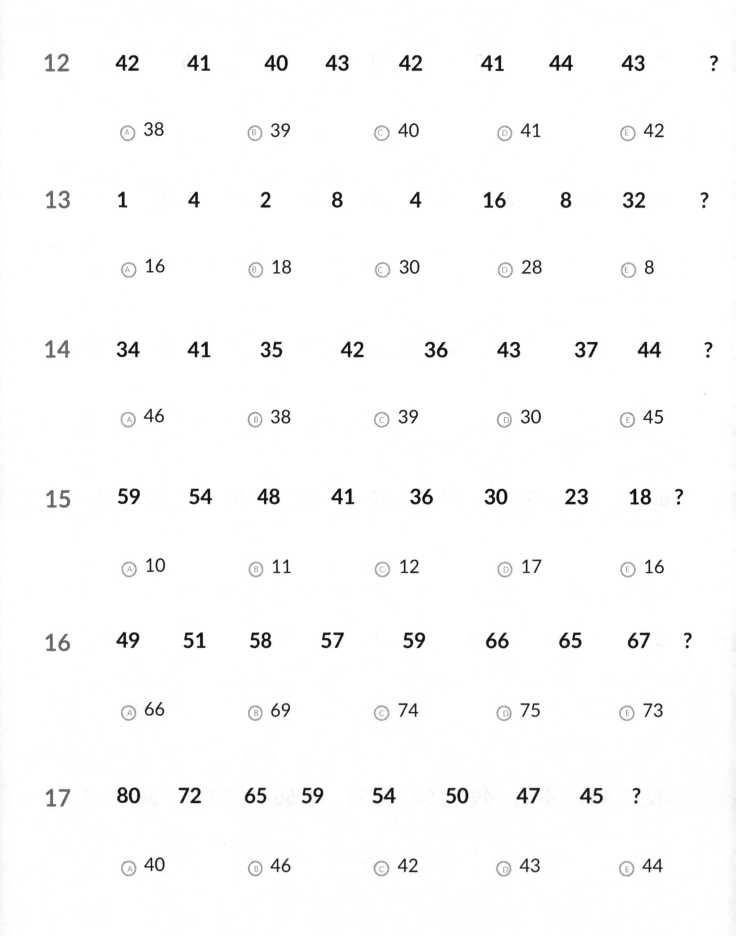

12   42   41   40   43   42   41   44   43   ?

     Ⓐ 38   Ⓑ 39   Ⓒ 40   Ⓓ 41   Ⓔ 42

13   1   4   2   8   4   16   8   32   ?

     Ⓐ 16   Ⓑ 18   Ⓒ 30   Ⓓ 28   Ⓔ 8

14   34   41   35   42   36   43   37   44   ?

     Ⓐ 46   Ⓑ 38   Ⓒ 39   Ⓓ 30   Ⓔ 45

15   59   54   48   41   36   30   23   18 ?

     Ⓐ 10   Ⓑ 11   Ⓒ 12   Ⓓ 17   Ⓔ 16

16   49   51   58   57   59   66   65   67   ?

     Ⓐ 66   Ⓑ 69   Ⓒ 74   Ⓓ 75   Ⓔ 73

17   80   72   65   59   54   50   47   45   ?

     Ⓐ 40   Ⓑ 46   Ⓒ 42   Ⓓ 43   Ⓔ 44

18   **52**   **19**   **53**   **20**   **54**   **21**   **55**   **22**   **56**   **?**

(A) 23   (B) 22   (C) 24   (D) 57   (E) 58

19   **0**   **1**   **2**   **4**   **5**   **6**   **12**   **13**   **14**   **28**   **?**

(A) 34   (B) 32   (C) 30   (D) 29   (E) 56

20   **51**   **-50**   **49**   **-48**   **47**   **-46**   **45**   **?**

(A) 44   (B) -44   (C) 43   (D) -43   (E) 46

21   **23**   **29**   **21**   **24**   **30**   **22**   **25**   **31**   **23**   **?**

(A) 36   (B) 15   (C) 28   (D) 29   (E) 26

22   **50**   **49**   **48**   **49**   **46**   **43**   **46**   **42**   **38**   **?**

(A) 38   (B) 46   (C) 45   (D) 42   (E) 44

23   **32**   **23**   **31**   **29**   **20**   **28**   **26**   **17**   **25**   **23**   **?**

(A) 21   (B) 31   (C) 14   (D) 15   (E) 22

- END OF PRACTICE TEST 2 -

PRACTICE TEST 1 ANSWER KEY

Compare these answers to what your child marked on the answer grid/bubble sheet.

Verbal Classification, Practice Test 1

_____ 1. E. cats   _____ 2. B. organs found inside body   _____ 3. E. types of non-fiction
_____ 4. A. verbs having to do with ending/concluding something
_____ 5. C. adjectives meaning not alike   _____ 6. D. continent adjectives
_____ 7. A. units of measure for time   _____ 8. C. yellow things
_____ 9. B. spherical shapes   _____ 10. C. having to do with making things less
_____ 11. E. places whose primary purpose is for people to walk on to go from one place to another
_____ 12. A. adjectives that describe not being enough   _____ 13. B. having to do with going down
_____ 14. C. having to do with being very wet   _____ 15. D. things under the ground
_____ 16. E. team/person one is competing against   _____ 17. A. places meant for storage
_____ 18. D. a geographical location with borders   _____ 19. B. jobs involved in building houses
_____ 20. E. adverbs having to do with frequency

Questions Answered Correctly: _____ out of 20

Verbal Analogies, Practice Test 1

_____ 1. C. a drum is a type of instrument; a horse is a type of mammal
_____ 2. E. letters put together make up words; sentences put together make up paragraphs
_____ 3. B. feet make a mile; days make a year
_____ 4. A. an enclosed space where dishes are stored is a cabinet; an enclosed space where hay is stored is a barn
_____ 5. D. homophones
_____ 6. E. both colors; both emotions associated with happiness
_____ 7. B. synonyms
_____ 8. A. if you add color to something, it becomes colorful; if you add water, it becomes wet
_____ 9. D. scientists conduct experiments to come to a conclusion; detectives conduct investigations to come to a conclusion
_____ 10. B. old-fashioned tool > modern tool to perform similar task (measuring time > doing math)
_____ 11. D. object > name of the middle of this object
_____ 12. E. both are precious metals > both are gases
_____ 13. A. synonyms
_____ 14. D. opposites
_____ 15. B. words where the letters are put in reverse order to form another word
_____ 16. E. sleeves extend out of a jacket; branches extend out of a tree
_____ 17. A. geography is a type of social studies; biology is a type of science
_____ 18. D. a chain is made of links; a fence is made of boards
_____ 19. E. A group of settlers forms a settlement. A group of ships forms a fleet.
_____ 20. D. when dirt is removed, an object becomes clean; when weight is removed, an object becomes light
_____ 21. A. things in numerical order are ordered by number; things in chronological order are ordered by time
_____ 22. E. Two wheels are on a bicycle. Two performers are in a duo.

Questions Answered Correctly: _____ out of 22

Sentence Completion, Practice Test 1

_____ 1. C. estimate: a rough count/calculation, not an exact one
_____ 2. A. introduction: the action of introducing
_____ 3. E. omit: to leave out
_____ 4. B. persuasive: able to make people do something or believe something
_____ 5. D. solution: an answer to a problem
_____ 6. A. tentative: not definite
_____ 7. E. treason: a crime of helping your country's enemies
_____ 8. D. random: chosen without a set plan
_____ 9. C. transmit: to send
_____ 10. A. verify: to make sure something is true/correct
_____ 11. B. inadequate: not enough
_____ 12. A. alternative: something that can be used in place of something else
_____ 13. E. disadvantage: something that makes things more difficult (the opposite of "advantage")
_____ 14. A. capable: able to do something
_____ 15. D. postpone: to move something to a later time
_____ 16. C. obsolete: replaced by something better/newer
_____ 17. B. originate: to come from
_____ 18. C. prosper: to become successful/healthy/strong
_____ 19. E. distinct: having differences that are easy to see   _____ 20. D. prominent: easily seen/noticed

Questions Answered Correctly: _____ out of 20

Figure Classification, Practice Test 1

_____ 1. D. inside larger shape are 2 small vertically-aligned squares with same color
_____ 2. A. same design inside (wavy lines)   _____ 3. E. trapezoids facing same direction
_____ 4. E. 7-sided shapes   _____ 5. D. rectangle & pentagon beside each other inside larger rectangle
_____ 6. A. there are 2 different kinds of shapes with 2 different designs inside - 1 is gray and 1 has wavy lines
_____ 7. B. inside larger shape are 3 squares: 1 black, 1 gray, 1 white   _____ 8. C. no rounded sides
_____ 9. E. on the top & bottom of the larger shape are 2 halves of the larger shape
_____ 10. D. half is black, half is gray
_____ 11. A. the bottom shape is the same as the top shape, but has been rotated 90° clockwise (to the right)
_____ 12. C. the middle shape has diagonal lines inside   _____ 13. B. inside circle is a trapezoid, circle, square, half circle
_____ 14. A. as the figures rotate, circle remains at same point on black shape -OR- the figures rotate 90° counterclockwise
_____ 15. B. same shapes inside square (triangle, rectangle, octagon)
_____ 16. E. in the group of 2 shapes, the second shape has 1 more side than the first
_____ 17. D. in the group of 2 shapes, the larger shape has 1 more side than the smaller shape
_____ 18. E. 1 crescent points up, 3 crescents point down
_____ 19. C. shape group consists of 1 half circle facing up, 1 triangle, 1 heart; there's 1 of each color (gray, white, or black)
_____ 20. D. shape group consists of 1 trapezoid, 1 triangle, 1 square; each must be a different color (gray, white, or black)
_____ 21. E. equilateral shapes (sides are same length)
_____ 22. B. small center shape & outer shape have the same design (or color) inside -and- the shapes are different kinds of shapes

Questions Answered Correctly: _____ out of 22

Figure Analogies, Practice Test 1

_____ 1. D. rotates 90° clockwise   _____ 2. B. shapes align vertically then switch colors
_____ 3. C. rotates 90° clockwise & 1 more design is added inside the outer square
_____ 4. E. bottom shape flips/rotates 180°, then the 2 shapes come together & the inner designs switch (vertical lines & black)
_____ 5. C. original shape becomes a shape with 1 more side
_____ 6. A. gray shape 'flips' down, white shape added on top that's facing the original position of the first shape
_____ 7. D. bottom shape becomes top shape & gets smaller, middle shape becomes bottom shape & gets bigger, top shape becomes middle shape & gets bigger
_____ 8. C. middle shape gets bigger, then top shape gets bigger & moves inside this shape, then bottom shape moves to the center of these two shapes and flips 180 degrees
_____ 9. E. middle shape becomes the largest outer shape; then, the top shape becomes the 2nd largest shape and moves inside the largest shape; then, the bottom shape moves inside both of these shapes, rotates 90° counterclockwise & turns gray
_____ 10. D. the gray of the inner shape & the vertical lines of the outer shape switch to outer shape & inner shape, respectively; outer shape adds +1 side
_____ 11. B. inside shape changes to a shape with +1 side; outside shape changes to a shape with +1 side; the new shapes switch colors black/white
_____ 12. C. shapes change like this: rectangles & triangles switch, ovals stay the same
_____ 13. D. in the sections of the squares/parallelograms, the colors/designs change like this: gray becomes filled with lines, black becomes gray, and sections filled with lines become black; also, the original figures do not change their shapes
_____ 14. B. the top left shape rotates 180°, the bottom right shape turns black & switches position with the top right shape
_____ 15. A. inside larger shapes are smaller shape in each of the corners which have 1 less side than the larger shape
_____ 16. B. smaller shape moves from lower left side to lower right side & lines inside smaller shape switch directions
_____ 17. D. the bottom shape becomes the largest outer shape; the top shape becomes larger & moves inside the largest shape; the middle shape moves inside the previous 2 shapes, then it rotates 90° clockwise
_____ 18. E. the shape group rotates 90° clockwise, then the gray circles become black and vice versa
_____ 19. A. the triangle with horizontal stripes becomes solid gray; the black triangle remains black; the triangle with dotted lines remains with dotted lines; then, the group of 3 triangles rotates 180°
_____ 20. E. each shape has 4 sections; there's a group of 4 shapes on the left and another group of 4 on the right; the sections that are black change from the left group of 4 shapes to the right group of 4 shapes, like this:
lower left >lower right; upper left > upper right; lower right> lower left; upper right > upper left
_____ 21. E. upper left figure rotates 180°; upper right & lower right shapes switch and the new upper right becomes black
_____ 22. C. color of large square changes from dark gray to white; top shape (triangle in top set, crescent in bottom set) rotates 180°; lower shapes (square, octagon in top set; oval, arrow in bottom set) switch sides -and- the bottom right shape (octagon in top set, arrow in bottom set) changes from filled with curvy lines to dark gray

Questions Answered Correctly: _____ out of 22

Paper Folding, Practice Test 1

_____ 1. E   _____ 2. D   _____ 3. C   _____ 4. B   _____ 5. C   _____ 6. D   _____ 7. A
_____ 8. E   _____ 9. B   _____ 10. C   _____ 11. B   _____ 12. A   _____ 13. C   _____ 14. D
_____ 15. B   _____ 16. D   _____ 17. C

Questions Answered Correctly: _____ out of 17

Number Puzzles, Practice Test 1

_____ 1. A   _____ 2. B   _____ 3. C   _____ 4. C   _____ 5. D   _____ 6. E   _____ 7. B   _____ 8. A
_____ 9. D   _____ 10. B   _____ 11. E   _____ 12. A   _____ 13. D   _____ 14. C   _____ 15. E   _____ 16. A
_____ 17. B

Questions Answered Correctly: _____ out of 17

Number Analogies, Practice Test 1

_____ 1. C. -18 _____ 2. E. +22 _____ 3. C. x9 _____ 4. D. ÷8 _____ 5. A. half
_____ 6. B. squared _____ 7. D. +1/5 _____ 8. E. ÷10 _____ 9. C. ÷11 _____ 10. E. same
_____ 11. E. +14 _____ 12. C. +32 _____ 13. B. ÷13 _____ 14. D. x2, then +1 _____ 15. D. x2, then -1
_____ 16. A. x3, then -1 _____ 17. E. x4, then +1 _____ 18. B. +14 _____ 19. C. ÷2, then +1
_____ 20. D. ÷2, then -1 _____ 21. D. ÷5, then +1 _____ 22. A. ÷3, then -1 _____ 23. C. x4, then +1

Questions Answered Correctly: _____ out of 23

Number Series, Practice Test 1

_____ 1.A. -17 _____ 2. C. x3
_____ 3. D. -1, -2, -1, -2, continues -OR- every other number is 3 less _____ 4. C. +1
_____ 5. B. 25-50-100 (repeats) _____ 6. D. -1, -2, -1, -2, continues -OR- every other number is 3 less
_____ 7. C. begins w/19, every other number is 19; then, starting with 52, every other number is +5
_____ 8. A. -11, -12, -13, -14, -15, etc. _____ 9. B. +14, +15, +16, +17, +18, etc.
_____ 10. C. -2, -4, -2, -4, continues -OR- every other number is 6 less
_____ 11. D. +1, +1, +2; +1, +1, +2, continues
_____ 12. C. the numbers in spaces 1, 3, 5, 7, 9 increase by 1; the numbers in spaces 2, 4, 6, 8, 10 increase by 1 -OR-
the difference in each pair of numbers is 11 (40 & 29; 41 & 30; 42 & 31, etc.)
_____ 13. E. x2, +1, repeats _____ 14. E. x4, ÷2, repeats -OR- every other number is doubled
_____ 15. A. +2, +2, -1, +2, +2, -1, etc. _____ 16. D. +3, -5, +7, +3, -5, +7, etc.
_____ 17. B. -5, +8, -6, -5, +8, -6, etc.
_____ 18. D. the numbers in spaces 1, 3, 5, 7, 9 decrease by 1; the numbers in spaces 2, 4, 6, 8, 10 increase by 1 -OR-
-25, +24, -23, +22, etc.
_____ 19. C. +1, +1, -1; +2, +2, -2; +3, +3, -3 _____ 20. A. x2, x2, ÷2; x2, x2, ÷2, etc.
_____ 21. E. the numbers in spaces 1, 3, 5, 7, 9 increase by 1; the numbers in spaces 2, 4, 6, 8, 10 increase by 1 -OR-
-6, +7, -6, +7, etc.
_____ 22. D. the numbers in spaces 1, 3, 5, 7, 9 increase by 1; the numbers in spaces 2, 4, 6, 8, 10 decrease by 1 -OR-
the difference between each pair of numbers increases by 2 (61-25=36; 62-24=38; 63-23=40, etc.)
_____ 23. B. +2, +3, +5; +2, +3, +5, etc.

Questions Answered Correctly: _____ out of 23

PRACTICE TEST 2 ANSWER KEY

Verbal Classification, Practice Test 2

_____ 1: C. planets _____ 2. D. types of performances _____ 3. B. countries
_____ 4. B. moving bodies of water _____ 5. A. adjectives to describe things that do not happen quickly
_____ 6. D. appliances used to cool things
_____ 7. A. fruits that grow on trees _____ 8. E. healthcare workers _____ 9. B. leaders
_____ 10. D. a thing that's identical to something else
_____ 11. E. having to do with bringing/mixing things together _____ 12. C. things that are green
_____ 13. A. different kinds of writers
_____ 14. E. parts of digestive system _____ 15. A. printed items that contain written information
_____ 16. E. used to carry/hold things _____ 17. C. used to describe sizes
_____ 18. B. verbs having to do with bringing things together
_____ 19. C. things that happen at the beginning of something (a story, a presidency, a life, the day)

Questions Answered Correctly: _____ out of 19

Verbal Analogies, Practice Test 2

_____ 1. B. a wrapper protects gum; bark protects a pine (tree type)
_____ 2. D. a tricycle has 3 wheels, a triangle has 3 sides
_____ 3. C. speed is measured by a speedometer; time is measured by a clock
_____ 4. A. sandpaper feels rough; a mirror feels smooth _____ 5. E. synonyms _____ 6. D. antonyms
_____ 7. B. the purpose of a freezer is to cool things inside; the purpose of a safe is to secure the things inside
_____ 8. B. present tense > past tense _____ 9. E. A very large wave is a tsunami. A very large building is a skyscraper.
_____ 10: C. A type of writer is a poet. A type of food is a pepper.
_____ 11. A. object > source of energy _____ 12. C. present time > in the past
_____ 13. D. a hoof is the foot of a giraffe; a paw is the foot of a rabbit
_____ 14. C. something that is bald has no hair; something that is dark has no light
_____ 15. E. a sock is a protective covering for a foot; an atmosphere is a protective covering for a planet (such as Earth)
_____ 16. B. this is an example of "degree"; something very dim is dark; something very cool is frigid
_____ 17. A. There is cooperation between partners. There is competition between opponents.
_____ 18. E. drought is caused by a lack of rain; hunger is caused by a lack of food
_____ 19. C. a telephone is used for communication; a plane is used for travel
_____ 20. B. you magnify with a lens; you cut with a blade
_____ 21. D. you use a magnifying glass to look at small things that are close; you use a telescope to look at large things that are
far away
_____ 22. C. a beaver works to create a dam; a journalist works to create a news story

Questions Answered Correctly: _____ out of 22

Sentence Completion, Practice Test 2

_____ 1. E. adapt: to change something so that it's easier to live in a particular place
_____ 2. C. flammable: catches fire easily _____ 3. A. consecutive: following one after another
_____ 4. B. slightly: with a very small amount _____ 5. D. plummet: to fall suddenly
_____ 6. E. treacherous: dangerous _____ 7. D. subtle: hard to see, not obvious
_____ 8. A. negotiate: to discuss something so that an agreement can be made
_____ 9. B. transform: to change something completely
_____ 10. D. modify: to change _____ 11. E. impartial: treating all equally
_____ 12. A. remote: far away from anything else
_____ 13. B. inhabitant: someone who lives in a particular place
_____ 14. C. dense: crowded; having things very close together
_____ 15. A. bias: to believe that a person/group/idea is better, resulting in unfair treatment of others
_____ 16. B. contribute: to give
_____ 17. C. priority: something that's more important than others and should be done first
_____ 18. D. acquire: to get _____ 19. A. authentic: real, not copied
_____ 20. E. emphasize: to put extra attention on

Questions Answered Correctly: _____ out of 20

Figure Classification, Practice Test 2

_____ 1. D. 6-sided shapes _____ 2. B. design inside triangles alternates lines/gray
_____ 3. D. 2 white shapes & 1 gray shape _____ 4. E. each shape group has a gray, dotted, and lined shape
_____ 5. A. # of shape sides = # of small shapes _____ 6. C. each group has a triangle, square, octagon
_____ 7. C. as triangle rotates, its sections remain in the same order
_____ 8. D. trapezoid is next to pac-man shape; a triangle is in another part of the grid
_____ 9. A. 8-sided shape with triangle inside shape
_____ 10. B. in circle are 3 shapes, 2 of which are the same (note, the same size), except 1 is gray
_____ 11. A. tic-tac-toe with parallelograms _____ 12. D. square divided into equal parts
_____ 13. C. the square is divided into 3 triangles; in the largest is a diamond; in the smaller 2 & on opposite sides as the diamond is a triangle & circle
_____ 14. E. each smaller shape is different _____ 15. B. an oval is between a heart and a rectangle
_____ 16. C. triangle has wavy lines that are aligned vertically
_____ 17. B. inner shape has one more side than outer shape
_____ 18. D. larger shape divided in half (dotted half/white half), white half has a small white version of larger shape
_____ 19. C. dotted shape has 1 more side than gray shape
_____ 20. B. one-quarter of shape has been "cut" _____ 21. D. star and heart are opposite each other (not directly beside)

Questions Answered Correctly: _____ out of 21

Figure Analogies, Practice Test 2

_____ 1. A. one more circle is added & the group rotates 90 degrees
_____ 2. E. one more shape is added & the group rotates 180 degrees
_____ 3. C. larger outer shape becomes the color of the smaller shape _____ 4. D. figure rotates 90 degrees counterclockwise
_____ 5. E. rectangle becomes square & diamond moves to the opposite side
_____ 6. B. top shape becomes larger & bottom shape moves inside; bottom shape rotates 90 degrees and a mirror image of this shape appears (it is facing the opposite direction)
_____ 7. A. crescents facing right become lined hearts; crescents facing down become triangles, crescents facing up become rectangles
_____ 8. B. large heart rotates 180 degrees; smaller hearts switch color _____ 9. E. mirror image of original figure
_____ 10. A. white shape turns black and rotates 90% counterclockwise; outside black shape disappears
_____ 11. A. upper left & lower right switch; upper right & lower left switch _____ 12. C. shape group rotates 180 degrees
_____ 13. B. R becomes O; O becomes R; M becomes L
_____ 14. C. in top set, square switches from white to wavy lines; the lower left triangle changes to a diamond, moves to the upper right, and the design inside changes from wavy lines to white; in the bottom, the reverse occurs; the square changes from wavy lines to white, the white triangle changes to a diamond, changes its position and design (white to wavy lines); no change w/ rectangle.
_____ 15. E. larger shape becomes shape with 2 more sides, smaller shape becomes shape with 1 more side; smaller & larger shape switch color
_____ 16. E. the outside shape becomes the inside shape, gets smaller, and switches color; the inside shape becomes the outside shape, gets bigger, and switches color; the middle shape remains the middle shape, gets smaller, and switches color
_____ 17. D. black becomes gray, gray becomes black, wavy lines remain the same
_____ 18. E. designs/colors change as follows: black becomes gray, vertical lines become black, gray becomes vertical lines; oval tilts opposite direction (changes from tilting to the right to tilting to the left)
_____ 19. C. in 2nd box, half of middle shape is covered; the gray section comes to the front while the white and black "quarters" switch positions with the gray section; the covered middle shape switches from white to dotted in the top set & from dotted to white on bottom set
_____ 20. D. group rotates 180 degrees & switches color
_____ 21. B. outer shape narrows and becomes black, inner shape gets bigger and forms a border around the other shape

Questions Answered Correctly: _____ out of 21

101

Paper Folding, Practice Test 2

_____ 1. D	_____ 2. B	_____ 3. A	_____ 4. E	_____ 5. D	_____ 6. C	_____ 7. E
_____ 8. C	_____ 9. D	_____ 10. D	_____ 11. E	_____ 12. B	_____ 13. A	_____ 14. B
_____ 15. B						

Questions Answered Correctly: _____ out of 15

Number Puzzles, Practice Test 2

_____ 1. A	_____ 2. E	_____ 3. B	_____ 4. D	_____ 5. A	_____ 6. B	_____ 7. C	_____ 8. D
_____ 9. A	_____ 10. E	_____ 11. E	_____ 12. B	_____ 13. A	_____ 14. C	_____ 15. B	_____ 16. D
_____ 17. C	_____ 18. D	_____ 19. A	_____ 20. B				

Questions Answered Correctly: _____ out of 20

Number Analogies, Practice Test 2

_____ 1. E. +38	_____ 2. A. x14	_____ 3. C. ÷12	_____ 4. D. half	_____ 5. B. squared
_____ 6. E. half	_____ 7. A. same	_____ 8. E. ÷10	_____ 9. C. ÷10	_____ 10. E. +33
_____ 11. D. x2 then +1	_____ 12. C. x5 then +1	_____ 13. B. x3 then -2	_____ 14. D. x4 then -1	_____ 15. A. -26
_____ 16. C. ÷9	_____ 17. C. ÷4 then +1	_____ 18. E. ÷2 then +1	_____ 19. E. same	_____ 20. A. x10
_____ 21. D. ÷3 then +1	_____ 22. B. ÷12	_____ 23. E. x4 then -1	_____ 24. B. ÷2 then +2	

Questions Answered Correctly: _____ out of 24

Number Series, Practice Test 2

_____ 1. A. +12   _____ 2. E. x2   _____ 3. C. +2.0   _____ 4. D. -1.0

_____ 5. B. every number repeats itself and then decreases by 2

_____ 6. A. begins w/7, every other number is 7; then, starting with 15, every other number is +10

_____ 7. B. +1, +8, +1, +8, continues -OR- every other number increases by 9

_____ 8. B. -2, -5, -2, -5, continues -OR- every other number decreases by 7

_____ 9. C. -1, -2, -3, -4, -5, etc.   _____ 10. A. 32, 16, 8, repeats   _____ 11. A. +1, +1, +5; +1, +1, +5, continues

_____ 12. E. -1, -1, +3; -1, -1, +3, continues

_____ 13. A. x4, then div. by 2 -OR- every other number is multiplied by 2

_____ 14. B. the numbers in spaces 1, 3, 5, 7, 9 increase by 1; the numbers in spaces 2, 4, 6, 8 increase by 1 -OR- +7, -6, +7, -6, etc.

_____ 15. C. -5,-6,-7, etc.   _____ 16. C. +2, +7, -1, repeats   _____ 17. E. -8, -7, -6, -5, -4, etc.

_____ 18. A. the numbers in spaces 1, 3, 5, 7, 9 increase by 1; the numbers in spaces 2, 4, 6, 8, 10 increase by 1 -OR- -33, +34, -33, +34, etc.

_____ 19. D. +1, +1, x2; +1, +1, x2, etc.

_____ 20. B. digits decrease by 1 (i.e., from 51 to 50 to 50 to 49, etc.) -AND- the signs alternate between positive and negative

_____ 21. E. +6, -8, +3, repeats

_____ 22. D. -1,-1,+1; -3,-3,+3; -4,-4,+4

_____ 23. C. -9, +8, -2, repeats

Questions Answered Correctly: _____ out of 23

- If this is your child's first time using COGAT-prep material, then do Practice Test 1 together, without assigning a time limit. (Skip the time limit suggestions below.)
- If this is <u>not</u> your child's first time using COGAT-prep material, then you may wish to have them do Practice Test 1 alone, following the steps below.
- Allow approximately 15 minutes for each section.
- Do a group of 3 question sections per day.
- Day 1, Verbal: 15 minutes each for Verbal Analogies, Verbal Classification, Sentence Completion = 45 minutes total
- Day 2, Non-Verbal: 15 minutes each for Figure Analogies, Figure Classification, Paper Folding = 45 minutes total
- Day 3, Quantitative: 15 minutes each for Number Analogies, Number Puzzles, Number Series = 45 minutes total
- After your child has completed Practice Test 1, go through the answer key to see which questions may not have been answered correctly. Go over the questions together that may have been missed.

Verbal Classification	Verbal Analogies	Sentence Completion	Figure Classification
1 Ⓐ Ⓑ Ⓒ Ⓓ Ⓔ	1 Ⓐ Ⓑ Ⓒ Ⓓ Ⓔ	1 Ⓐ Ⓑ Ⓒ Ⓓ Ⓔ	1 Ⓐ Ⓑ Ⓒ Ⓓ Ⓔ
2 Ⓐ Ⓑ Ⓒ Ⓓ Ⓔ	2 Ⓐ Ⓑ Ⓒ Ⓓ Ⓔ	2 Ⓐ Ⓑ Ⓒ Ⓓ Ⓔ	2 Ⓐ Ⓑ Ⓒ Ⓓ Ⓔ
3 Ⓐ Ⓑ Ⓒ Ⓓ Ⓔ	3 Ⓐ Ⓑ Ⓒ Ⓓ Ⓔ	3 Ⓐ Ⓑ Ⓒ Ⓓ Ⓔ	3 Ⓐ Ⓑ Ⓒ Ⓓ Ⓔ
4 Ⓐ Ⓑ Ⓒ Ⓓ Ⓔ	4 Ⓐ Ⓑ Ⓒ Ⓓ Ⓔ	4 Ⓐ Ⓑ Ⓒ Ⓓ Ⓔ	4 Ⓐ Ⓑ Ⓒ Ⓓ Ⓔ
5 Ⓐ Ⓑ Ⓒ Ⓓ Ⓔ	5 Ⓐ Ⓑ Ⓒ Ⓓ Ⓔ	5 Ⓐ Ⓑ Ⓒ Ⓓ Ⓔ	5 Ⓐ Ⓑ Ⓒ Ⓓ Ⓔ
6 Ⓐ Ⓑ Ⓒ Ⓓ Ⓔ	6 Ⓐ Ⓑ Ⓒ Ⓓ Ⓔ	6 Ⓐ Ⓑ Ⓒ Ⓓ Ⓔ	6 Ⓐ Ⓑ Ⓒ Ⓓ Ⓔ
7 Ⓐ Ⓑ Ⓒ Ⓓ Ⓔ	7 Ⓐ Ⓑ Ⓒ Ⓓ Ⓔ	7 Ⓐ Ⓑ Ⓒ Ⓓ Ⓔ	7 Ⓐ Ⓑ Ⓒ Ⓓ Ⓔ
8 Ⓐ Ⓑ Ⓒ Ⓓ Ⓔ	8 Ⓐ Ⓑ Ⓒ Ⓓ Ⓔ	8 Ⓐ Ⓑ Ⓒ Ⓓ Ⓔ	8 Ⓐ Ⓑ Ⓒ Ⓓ Ⓔ
9 Ⓐ Ⓑ Ⓒ Ⓓ Ⓔ	9 Ⓐ Ⓑ Ⓒ Ⓓ Ⓔ	9 Ⓐ Ⓑ Ⓒ Ⓓ Ⓔ	9 Ⓐ Ⓑ Ⓒ Ⓓ Ⓔ
10 Ⓐ Ⓑ Ⓒ Ⓓ Ⓔ	10 Ⓐ Ⓑ Ⓒ Ⓓ Ⓔ	10 Ⓐ Ⓑ Ⓒ Ⓓ Ⓔ	10 Ⓐ Ⓑ Ⓒ Ⓓ Ⓔ
11 Ⓐ Ⓑ Ⓒ Ⓓ Ⓔ	11 Ⓐ Ⓑ Ⓒ Ⓓ Ⓔ	11 Ⓐ Ⓑ Ⓒ Ⓓ Ⓔ	11 Ⓐ Ⓑ Ⓒ Ⓓ Ⓔ
12 Ⓐ Ⓑ Ⓒ Ⓓ Ⓔ	12 Ⓐ Ⓑ Ⓒ Ⓓ Ⓔ	12 Ⓐ Ⓑ Ⓒ Ⓓ Ⓔ	12 Ⓐ Ⓑ Ⓒ Ⓓ Ⓔ
13 Ⓐ Ⓑ Ⓒ Ⓓ Ⓔ	13 Ⓐ Ⓑ Ⓒ Ⓓ Ⓔ	13 Ⓐ Ⓑ Ⓒ Ⓓ Ⓔ	13 Ⓐ Ⓑ Ⓒ Ⓓ Ⓔ
14 Ⓐ Ⓑ Ⓒ Ⓓ Ⓔ	14 Ⓐ Ⓑ Ⓒ Ⓓ Ⓔ	14 Ⓐ Ⓑ Ⓒ Ⓓ Ⓔ	14 Ⓐ Ⓑ Ⓒ Ⓓ Ⓔ
15 Ⓐ Ⓑ Ⓒ Ⓓ Ⓔ	15 Ⓐ Ⓑ Ⓒ Ⓓ Ⓔ	15 Ⓐ Ⓑ Ⓒ Ⓓ Ⓔ	15 Ⓐ Ⓑ Ⓒ Ⓓ Ⓔ
16 Ⓐ Ⓑ Ⓒ Ⓓ Ⓔ	16 Ⓐ Ⓑ Ⓒ Ⓓ Ⓔ	16 Ⓐ Ⓑ Ⓒ Ⓓ Ⓔ	16 Ⓐ Ⓑ Ⓒ Ⓓ Ⓔ
17 Ⓐ Ⓑ Ⓒ Ⓓ Ⓔ	17 Ⓐ Ⓑ Ⓒ Ⓓ Ⓔ	17 Ⓐ Ⓑ Ⓒ Ⓓ Ⓔ	17 Ⓐ Ⓑ Ⓒ Ⓓ Ⓔ
18 Ⓐ Ⓑ Ⓒ Ⓓ Ⓔ	18 Ⓐ Ⓑ Ⓒ Ⓓ Ⓔ	18 Ⓐ Ⓑ Ⓒ Ⓓ Ⓔ	18 Ⓐ Ⓑ Ⓒ Ⓓ Ⓔ
19 Ⓐ Ⓑ Ⓒ Ⓓ Ⓔ	19 Ⓐ Ⓑ Ⓒ Ⓓ Ⓔ	19 Ⓐ Ⓑ Ⓒ Ⓓ Ⓔ	19 Ⓐ Ⓑ Ⓒ Ⓓ Ⓔ
20 Ⓐ Ⓑ Ⓒ Ⓓ Ⓔ	20 Ⓐ Ⓑ Ⓒ Ⓓ Ⓔ	20 Ⓐ Ⓑ Ⓒ Ⓓ Ⓔ	20 Ⓐ Ⓑ Ⓒ Ⓓ Ⓔ
	21 Ⓐ Ⓑ Ⓒ Ⓓ Ⓔ		21 Ⓐ Ⓑ Ⓒ Ⓓ Ⓔ
	22 Ⓐ Ⓑ Ⓒ Ⓓ Ⓔ		22 Ⓐ Ⓑ Ⓒ Ⓓ Ⓔ

Figure Analogies

1 Ⓐ Ⓑ Ⓒ Ⓓ Ⓔ
2 Ⓐ Ⓑ Ⓒ Ⓓ Ⓔ
3 Ⓐ Ⓑ Ⓒ Ⓓ Ⓔ
4 Ⓐ Ⓑ Ⓒ Ⓓ Ⓔ
5 Ⓐ Ⓑ Ⓒ Ⓓ Ⓔ
6 Ⓐ Ⓑ Ⓒ Ⓓ Ⓔ
7 Ⓐ Ⓑ Ⓒ Ⓓ Ⓔ
8 Ⓐ Ⓑ Ⓒ Ⓓ Ⓔ
9 Ⓐ Ⓑ Ⓒ Ⓓ Ⓔ
10 Ⓐ Ⓑ Ⓒ Ⓓ Ⓔ
11 Ⓐ Ⓑ Ⓒ Ⓓ Ⓔ
12 Ⓐ Ⓑ Ⓒ Ⓓ Ⓔ
13 Ⓐ Ⓑ Ⓒ Ⓓ Ⓔ
14 Ⓐ Ⓑ Ⓒ Ⓓ Ⓔ
15 Ⓐ Ⓑ Ⓒ Ⓓ Ⓔ
16 Ⓐ Ⓑ Ⓒ Ⓓ Ⓔ
17 Ⓐ Ⓑ Ⓒ Ⓓ Ⓔ
18 Ⓐ Ⓑ Ⓒ Ⓓ Ⓔ
19 Ⓐ Ⓑ Ⓒ Ⓓ Ⓔ
20 Ⓐ Ⓑ Ⓒ Ⓓ Ⓔ
21 Ⓐ Ⓑ Ⓒ Ⓓ Ⓔ
22 Ⓐ Ⓑ Ⓒ Ⓓ Ⓔ

Paper Folding

1 Ⓐ Ⓑ Ⓒ Ⓓ Ⓔ
2 Ⓐ Ⓑ Ⓒ Ⓓ Ⓔ
3 Ⓐ Ⓑ Ⓒ Ⓓ Ⓔ
4 Ⓐ Ⓑ Ⓒ Ⓓ Ⓔ
5 Ⓐ Ⓑ Ⓒ Ⓓ Ⓔ
6 Ⓐ Ⓑ Ⓒ Ⓓ Ⓔ
7 Ⓐ Ⓑ Ⓒ Ⓓ Ⓔ
8 Ⓐ Ⓑ Ⓒ Ⓓ Ⓔ
9 Ⓐ Ⓑ Ⓒ Ⓓ Ⓔ
10 Ⓐ Ⓑ Ⓒ Ⓓ Ⓔ
11 Ⓐ Ⓑ Ⓒ Ⓓ Ⓔ
12 Ⓐ Ⓑ Ⓒ Ⓓ Ⓔ
13 Ⓐ Ⓑ Ⓒ Ⓓ Ⓔ
14 Ⓐ Ⓑ Ⓒ Ⓓ Ⓔ
15 Ⓐ Ⓑ Ⓒ Ⓓ Ⓔ
16 Ⓐ Ⓑ Ⓒ Ⓓ Ⓔ
17 Ⓐ Ⓑ Ⓒ Ⓓ Ⓔ

Number Puzzles

1 Ⓐ Ⓑ Ⓒ Ⓓ Ⓔ
2 Ⓐ Ⓑ Ⓒ Ⓓ Ⓔ
3 Ⓐ Ⓑ Ⓒ Ⓓ Ⓔ
4 Ⓐ Ⓑ Ⓒ Ⓓ Ⓔ
5 Ⓐ Ⓑ Ⓒ Ⓓ Ⓔ
6 Ⓐ Ⓑ Ⓒ Ⓓ Ⓔ
7 Ⓐ Ⓑ Ⓒ Ⓓ Ⓔ
8 Ⓐ Ⓑ Ⓒ Ⓓ Ⓔ
9 Ⓐ Ⓑ Ⓒ Ⓓ Ⓔ
10 Ⓐ Ⓑ Ⓒ Ⓓ Ⓔ
11 Ⓐ Ⓑ Ⓒ Ⓓ Ⓔ
12 Ⓐ Ⓑ Ⓒ Ⓓ Ⓔ
13 Ⓐ Ⓑ Ⓒ Ⓓ Ⓔ
14 Ⓐ Ⓑ Ⓒ Ⓓ Ⓔ
15 Ⓐ Ⓑ Ⓒ Ⓓ Ⓔ
16 Ⓐ Ⓑ Ⓒ Ⓓ Ⓔ
17 Ⓐ Ⓑ Ⓒ Ⓓ Ⓔ

Number Analogies

1 Ⓐ Ⓑ Ⓒ Ⓓ Ⓔ
2 Ⓐ Ⓑ Ⓒ Ⓓ Ⓔ
3 Ⓐ Ⓑ Ⓒ Ⓓ Ⓔ
4 Ⓐ Ⓑ Ⓒ Ⓓ Ⓔ
5 Ⓐ Ⓑ Ⓒ Ⓓ Ⓔ
6 Ⓐ Ⓑ Ⓒ Ⓓ Ⓔ
7 Ⓐ Ⓑ Ⓒ Ⓓ Ⓔ
8 Ⓐ Ⓑ Ⓒ Ⓓ Ⓔ
9 Ⓐ Ⓑ Ⓒ Ⓓ Ⓔ
10 Ⓐ Ⓑ Ⓒ Ⓓ Ⓔ
11 Ⓐ Ⓑ Ⓒ Ⓓ Ⓔ
12 Ⓐ Ⓑ Ⓒ Ⓓ Ⓔ
13 Ⓐ Ⓑ Ⓒ Ⓓ Ⓔ
14 Ⓐ Ⓑ Ⓒ Ⓓ Ⓔ
15 Ⓐ Ⓑ Ⓒ Ⓓ Ⓔ
16 Ⓐ Ⓑ Ⓒ Ⓓ Ⓔ
17 Ⓐ Ⓑ Ⓒ Ⓓ Ⓔ
18 Ⓐ Ⓑ Ⓒ Ⓓ Ⓔ
19 Ⓐ Ⓑ Ⓒ Ⓓ Ⓔ
20 Ⓐ Ⓑ Ⓒ Ⓓ Ⓔ
21 Ⓐ Ⓑ Ⓒ Ⓓ Ⓔ
22 Ⓐ Ⓑ Ⓒ Ⓓ Ⓔ
23 Ⓐ Ⓑ Ⓒ Ⓓ Ⓔ

Number Series

1 Ⓐ Ⓑ Ⓒ Ⓓ Ⓔ
2 Ⓐ Ⓑ Ⓒ Ⓓ Ⓔ
3 Ⓐ Ⓑ Ⓒ Ⓓ Ⓔ
4 Ⓐ Ⓑ Ⓒ Ⓓ Ⓔ
5 Ⓐ Ⓑ Ⓒ Ⓓ Ⓔ
6 Ⓐ Ⓑ Ⓒ Ⓓ Ⓔ
7 Ⓐ Ⓑ Ⓒ Ⓓ Ⓔ
8 Ⓐ Ⓑ Ⓒ Ⓓ Ⓔ
9 Ⓐ Ⓑ Ⓒ Ⓓ Ⓔ
10 Ⓐ Ⓑ Ⓒ Ⓓ Ⓔ
11 Ⓐ Ⓑ Ⓒ Ⓓ Ⓔ
12 Ⓐ Ⓑ Ⓒ Ⓓ Ⓔ
13 Ⓐ Ⓑ Ⓒ Ⓓ Ⓔ
14 Ⓐ Ⓑ Ⓒ Ⓓ Ⓔ
15 Ⓐ Ⓑ Ⓒ Ⓓ Ⓔ
16 Ⓐ Ⓑ Ⓒ Ⓓ Ⓔ
17 Ⓐ Ⓑ Ⓒ Ⓓ Ⓔ
18 Ⓐ Ⓑ Ⓒ Ⓓ Ⓔ
19 Ⓐ Ⓑ Ⓒ Ⓓ Ⓔ
20 Ⓐ Ⓑ Ⓒ Ⓓ Ⓔ
21 Ⓐ Ⓑ Ⓒ Ⓓ Ⓔ
22 Ⓐ Ⓑ Ⓒ Ⓓ Ⓔ
23 Ⓐ Ⓑ Ⓒ Ⓓ Ⓔ

PRACTICE TEST 2 ANSWER GRID/BUBBLE SHEET

- After completing Practice Test 1, have your child complete Practice Test 2 on his/her own.
- (Do not tell whether the answers are correct or not until the test is completed).
- Assign a time limit for each of the 9 question sections (Verbal Analogies, Verbal Classification, etc.) of around 15 minutes each.

Complete a group of 3 question sections per day. For example:

- Day 1, Verbal: 15 minutes each for Verbal Analogies, Verbal Classification, Sentence Completion = 45 minutes total
- Day 2, Non-Verbal: 15 minutes each for Figure Analogies, Figure Classification, Paper Folding = 45 minutes total
- Day 3, Quantitative: 15 minutes each for Number Analogies, Number Puzzles, Number Series = 45 minutes total
- After your student is finished, on your own (without your child), go through the answer key by question type to see which answers were correct/incorrect. Then, go over any missed questions with your child.

Verbal Classification	Verbal Analogies	Sentence Completion	Figure Classification
1 Ⓐ Ⓑ Ⓒ Ⓓ Ⓔ	1 Ⓐ Ⓑ Ⓒ Ⓓ Ⓔ	1 Ⓐ Ⓑ Ⓒ Ⓓ Ⓔ	1 Ⓐ Ⓑ Ⓒ Ⓓ Ⓔ
2 Ⓐ Ⓑ Ⓒ Ⓓ Ⓔ	2 Ⓐ Ⓑ Ⓒ Ⓓ Ⓔ	2 Ⓐ Ⓑ Ⓒ Ⓓ Ⓔ	2 Ⓐ Ⓑ Ⓒ Ⓓ Ⓔ
3 Ⓐ Ⓑ Ⓒ Ⓓ Ⓔ	3 Ⓐ Ⓑ Ⓒ Ⓓ Ⓔ	3 Ⓐ Ⓑ Ⓒ Ⓓ Ⓔ	3 Ⓐ Ⓑ Ⓒ Ⓓ Ⓔ
4 Ⓐ Ⓑ Ⓒ Ⓓ Ⓔ	4 Ⓐ Ⓑ Ⓒ Ⓓ Ⓔ	4 Ⓐ Ⓑ Ⓒ Ⓓ Ⓔ	4 Ⓐ Ⓑ Ⓒ Ⓓ Ⓔ
5 Ⓐ Ⓑ Ⓒ Ⓓ Ⓔ	5 Ⓐ Ⓑ Ⓒ Ⓓ Ⓔ	5 Ⓐ Ⓑ Ⓒ Ⓓ Ⓔ	5 Ⓐ Ⓑ Ⓒ Ⓓ Ⓔ
6 Ⓐ Ⓑ Ⓒ Ⓓ Ⓔ	6 Ⓐ Ⓑ Ⓒ Ⓓ Ⓔ	6 Ⓐ Ⓑ Ⓒ Ⓓ Ⓔ	6 Ⓐ Ⓑ Ⓒ Ⓓ Ⓔ
7 Ⓐ Ⓑ Ⓒ Ⓓ Ⓔ	7 Ⓐ Ⓑ Ⓒ Ⓓ Ⓔ	7 Ⓐ Ⓑ Ⓒ Ⓓ Ⓔ	7 Ⓐ Ⓑ Ⓒ Ⓓ Ⓔ
8 Ⓐ Ⓑ Ⓒ Ⓓ Ⓔ	8 Ⓐ Ⓑ Ⓒ Ⓓ Ⓔ	8 Ⓐ Ⓑ Ⓒ Ⓓ Ⓔ	8 Ⓐ Ⓑ Ⓒ Ⓓ Ⓔ
9 Ⓐ Ⓑ Ⓒ Ⓓ Ⓔ	9 Ⓐ Ⓑ Ⓒ Ⓓ Ⓔ	9 Ⓐ Ⓑ Ⓒ Ⓓ Ⓔ	9 Ⓐ Ⓑ Ⓒ Ⓓ Ⓔ
10 Ⓐ Ⓑ Ⓒ Ⓓ Ⓔ	10 Ⓐ Ⓑ Ⓒ Ⓓ Ⓔ	10 Ⓐ Ⓑ Ⓒ Ⓓ Ⓔ	10 Ⓐ Ⓑ Ⓒ Ⓓ Ⓔ
11 Ⓐ Ⓑ Ⓒ Ⓓ Ⓔ	11 Ⓐ Ⓑ Ⓒ Ⓓ Ⓔ	11 Ⓐ Ⓑ Ⓒ Ⓓ Ⓔ	11 Ⓐ Ⓑ Ⓒ Ⓓ Ⓔ
12 Ⓐ Ⓑ Ⓒ Ⓓ Ⓔ	12 Ⓐ Ⓑ Ⓒ Ⓓ Ⓔ	12 Ⓐ Ⓑ Ⓒ Ⓓ Ⓔ	12 Ⓐ Ⓑ Ⓒ Ⓓ Ⓔ
13 Ⓐ Ⓑ Ⓒ Ⓓ Ⓔ	13 Ⓐ Ⓑ Ⓒ Ⓓ Ⓔ	13 Ⓐ Ⓑ Ⓒ Ⓓ Ⓔ	13 Ⓐ Ⓑ Ⓒ Ⓓ Ⓔ
14 Ⓐ Ⓑ Ⓒ Ⓓ Ⓔ	14 Ⓐ Ⓑ Ⓒ Ⓓ Ⓔ	14 Ⓐ Ⓑ Ⓒ Ⓓ Ⓔ	14 Ⓐ Ⓑ Ⓒ Ⓓ Ⓔ
15 Ⓐ Ⓑ Ⓒ Ⓓ Ⓔ	15 Ⓐ Ⓑ Ⓒ Ⓓ Ⓔ	15 Ⓐ Ⓑ Ⓒ Ⓓ Ⓔ	15 Ⓐ Ⓑ Ⓒ Ⓓ Ⓔ
16 Ⓐ Ⓑ Ⓒ Ⓓ Ⓔ	16 Ⓐ Ⓑ Ⓒ Ⓓ Ⓔ	16 Ⓐ Ⓑ Ⓒ Ⓓ Ⓔ	16 Ⓐ Ⓑ Ⓒ Ⓓ Ⓔ
17 Ⓐ Ⓑ Ⓒ Ⓓ Ⓔ	17 Ⓐ Ⓑ Ⓒ Ⓓ Ⓔ	17 Ⓐ Ⓑ Ⓒ Ⓓ Ⓔ	17 Ⓐ Ⓑ Ⓒ Ⓓ Ⓔ
18 Ⓐ Ⓑ Ⓒ Ⓓ Ⓔ	18 Ⓐ Ⓑ Ⓒ Ⓓ Ⓔ	18 Ⓐ Ⓑ Ⓒ Ⓓ Ⓔ	18 Ⓐ Ⓑ Ⓒ Ⓓ Ⓔ
19 Ⓐ Ⓑ Ⓒ Ⓓ Ⓔ	19 Ⓐ Ⓑ Ⓒ Ⓓ Ⓔ	19 Ⓐ Ⓑ Ⓒ Ⓓ Ⓔ	19 Ⓐ Ⓑ Ⓒ Ⓓ Ⓔ
	20 Ⓐ Ⓑ Ⓒ Ⓓ Ⓔ	20 Ⓐ Ⓑ Ⓒ Ⓓ Ⓔ	20 Ⓐ Ⓑ Ⓒ Ⓓ Ⓔ
	21 Ⓐ Ⓑ Ⓒ Ⓓ Ⓔ		21 Ⓐ Ⓑ Ⓒ Ⓓ Ⓔ
	22 Ⓐ Ⓑ Ⓒ Ⓓ Ⓔ		

Figure Analogies

1 Ⓐ Ⓑ Ⓒ Ⓓ Ⓔ
2 Ⓐ Ⓑ Ⓒ Ⓓ Ⓔ
3 Ⓐ Ⓑ Ⓒ Ⓓ Ⓔ
4 Ⓐ Ⓑ Ⓒ Ⓓ Ⓔ
5 Ⓐ Ⓑ Ⓒ Ⓓ Ⓔ
6 Ⓐ Ⓑ Ⓒ Ⓓ Ⓔ
7 Ⓐ Ⓑ Ⓒ Ⓓ Ⓔ
8 Ⓐ Ⓑ Ⓒ Ⓓ Ⓔ
9 Ⓐ Ⓑ Ⓒ Ⓓ Ⓔ
10 Ⓐ Ⓑ Ⓒ Ⓓ Ⓔ
11 Ⓐ Ⓑ Ⓒ Ⓓ Ⓔ
12 Ⓐ Ⓑ Ⓒ Ⓓ Ⓔ
13 Ⓐ Ⓑ Ⓒ Ⓓ Ⓔ
14 Ⓐ Ⓑ Ⓒ Ⓓ Ⓔ
15 Ⓐ Ⓑ Ⓒ Ⓓ Ⓔ
16 Ⓐ Ⓑ Ⓒ Ⓓ Ⓔ
17 Ⓐ Ⓑ Ⓒ Ⓓ Ⓔ
18 Ⓐ Ⓑ Ⓒ Ⓓ Ⓔ
19 Ⓐ Ⓑ Ⓒ Ⓓ Ⓔ
20 Ⓐ Ⓑ Ⓒ Ⓓ Ⓔ
21 Ⓐ Ⓑ Ⓒ Ⓓ Ⓔ

Paper Folding

1 Ⓐ Ⓑ Ⓒ Ⓓ Ⓔ
2 Ⓐ Ⓑ Ⓒ Ⓓ Ⓔ
3 Ⓐ Ⓑ Ⓒ Ⓓ Ⓔ
4 Ⓐ Ⓑ Ⓒ Ⓓ Ⓔ
5 Ⓐ Ⓑ Ⓒ Ⓓ Ⓔ
6 Ⓐ Ⓑ Ⓒ Ⓓ Ⓔ
7 Ⓐ Ⓑ Ⓒ Ⓓ Ⓔ
8 Ⓐ Ⓑ Ⓒ Ⓓ Ⓔ
9 Ⓐ Ⓑ Ⓒ Ⓓ Ⓔ
10 Ⓐ Ⓑ Ⓒ Ⓓ Ⓔ
11 Ⓐ Ⓑ Ⓒ Ⓓ Ⓔ
12 Ⓐ Ⓑ Ⓒ Ⓓ Ⓔ
13 Ⓐ Ⓑ Ⓒ Ⓓ Ⓔ
14 Ⓐ Ⓑ Ⓒ Ⓓ Ⓔ
15 Ⓐ Ⓑ Ⓒ Ⓓ Ⓔ

Number Puzzles

1 Ⓐ Ⓑ Ⓒ Ⓓ Ⓔ
2 Ⓐ Ⓑ Ⓒ Ⓓ Ⓔ
3 Ⓐ Ⓑ Ⓒ Ⓓ Ⓔ
4 Ⓐ Ⓑ Ⓒ Ⓓ Ⓔ
5 Ⓐ Ⓑ Ⓒ Ⓓ Ⓔ
6 Ⓐ Ⓑ Ⓒ Ⓓ Ⓔ
7 Ⓐ Ⓑ Ⓒ Ⓓ Ⓔ
8 Ⓐ Ⓑ Ⓒ Ⓓ Ⓔ
9 Ⓐ Ⓑ Ⓒ Ⓓ Ⓔ
10 Ⓐ Ⓑ Ⓒ Ⓓ Ⓔ
11 Ⓐ Ⓑ Ⓒ Ⓓ Ⓔ
12 Ⓐ Ⓑ Ⓒ Ⓓ Ⓔ
13 Ⓐ Ⓑ Ⓒ Ⓓ Ⓔ
14 Ⓐ Ⓑ Ⓒ Ⓓ Ⓔ
15 Ⓐ Ⓑ Ⓒ Ⓓ Ⓔ
16 Ⓐ Ⓑ Ⓒ Ⓓ Ⓔ
17 Ⓐ Ⓑ Ⓒ Ⓓ Ⓔ
18 Ⓐ Ⓑ Ⓒ Ⓓ Ⓔ
19 Ⓐ Ⓑ Ⓒ Ⓓ Ⓔ
20 Ⓐ Ⓑ Ⓒ Ⓓ Ⓔ

Number Analogies

1 Ⓐ Ⓑ Ⓒ Ⓓ Ⓔ
2 Ⓐ Ⓑ Ⓒ Ⓓ Ⓔ
3 Ⓐ Ⓑ Ⓒ Ⓓ Ⓔ
4 Ⓐ Ⓑ Ⓒ Ⓓ Ⓔ
5 Ⓐ Ⓑ Ⓒ Ⓓ Ⓔ
6 Ⓐ Ⓑ Ⓒ Ⓓ Ⓔ
7 Ⓐ Ⓑ Ⓒ Ⓓ Ⓔ
8 Ⓐ Ⓑ Ⓒ Ⓓ Ⓔ
9 Ⓐ Ⓑ Ⓒ Ⓓ Ⓔ
10 Ⓐ Ⓑ Ⓒ Ⓓ Ⓔ
11 Ⓐ Ⓑ Ⓒ Ⓓ Ⓔ
12 Ⓐ Ⓑ Ⓒ Ⓓ Ⓔ
13 Ⓐ Ⓑ Ⓒ Ⓓ Ⓔ
14 Ⓐ Ⓑ Ⓒ Ⓓ Ⓔ
15 Ⓐ Ⓑ Ⓒ Ⓓ Ⓔ
16 Ⓐ Ⓑ Ⓒ Ⓓ Ⓔ
17 Ⓐ Ⓑ Ⓒ Ⓓ Ⓔ
18 Ⓐ Ⓑ Ⓒ Ⓓ Ⓔ
19 Ⓐ Ⓑ Ⓒ Ⓓ Ⓔ
20 Ⓐ Ⓑ Ⓒ Ⓓ Ⓔ
21 Ⓐ Ⓑ Ⓒ Ⓓ Ⓔ
22 Ⓐ Ⓑ Ⓒ Ⓓ Ⓔ
23 Ⓐ Ⓑ Ⓒ Ⓓ Ⓔ
24 Ⓐ Ⓑ Ⓒ Ⓓ Ⓔ

Number Series

1 Ⓐ Ⓑ Ⓒ Ⓓ Ⓔ
2 Ⓐ Ⓑ Ⓒ Ⓓ Ⓔ
3 Ⓐ Ⓑ Ⓒ Ⓓ Ⓔ
4 Ⓐ Ⓑ Ⓒ Ⓓ Ⓔ
5 Ⓐ Ⓑ Ⓒ Ⓓ Ⓔ
6 Ⓐ Ⓑ Ⓒ Ⓓ Ⓔ
7 Ⓐ Ⓑ Ⓒ Ⓓ Ⓔ
8 Ⓐ Ⓑ Ⓒ Ⓓ Ⓔ
9 Ⓐ Ⓑ Ⓒ Ⓓ Ⓔ
10 Ⓐ Ⓑ Ⓒ Ⓓ Ⓔ
11 Ⓐ Ⓑ Ⓒ Ⓓ Ⓔ
12 Ⓐ Ⓑ Ⓒ Ⓓ Ⓔ
13 Ⓐ Ⓑ Ⓒ Ⓓ Ⓔ
14 Ⓐ Ⓑ Ⓒ Ⓓ Ⓔ
15 Ⓐ Ⓑ Ⓒ Ⓓ Ⓔ
16 Ⓐ Ⓑ Ⓒ Ⓓ Ⓔ
17 Ⓐ Ⓑ Ⓒ Ⓓ Ⓔ
18 Ⓐ Ⓑ Ⓒ Ⓓ Ⓔ
19 Ⓐ Ⓑ Ⓒ Ⓓ Ⓔ
20 Ⓐ Ⓑ Ⓒ Ⓓ Ⓔ
21 Ⓐ Ⓑ Ⓒ Ⓓ Ⓔ
22 Ⓐ Ⓑ Ⓒ Ⓓ Ⓔ
23 Ⓐ Ⓑ Ⓒ Ⓓ Ⓔ

Made in the USA
Middletown, DE
11 October 2023

40633235R10060